Good Luck Bill

Carrie Herzner

DEDICATION

For Katie and Twig.

CONTENTS

ACKNOWLEDGMENTS

First and foremost, I must thank Bill, for granting me permission to share our story.

Very special thanks to Ariel Gore and her School for Wayward Writers; and to Jerry Dennis and the Antioch Writers' Workshop. Thank you to everyone who read early drafts: Carol Feiser Laque, Bucky Ignatius, Susan Glassmeyer, Julie Hollyday, and Andrea Jagello—thank you for being so generous with your time and honest in your critique. Thank you to those who gave their blessings and encouragement: Fixer, Kentucky, Shakespeare, Mom, Katie, Twig. Thank you to Trish McKinnley and Diana Johnston for your spiritual guidance and emotional support. Thank you to Melissa Class Rudy—you are an angel, and the editor of my dreams. I wasn't kidding when I said every time I think of you, "You're Every Woman in the World" by Air Supply plays through my head. Thank you to Rob E. Boley, for all your advice and professional insight. Thank you to Brandon Losacker, for your beautifully haunting cover design, book trailer, and all the work you do behind the scenes.

To my children—you have taught me that the human heart is capable of infinite expansion and love.

I've always been enchanted by Greek Mythology, so a special shout-out goes to Apollo, the god of music, truth, prophecy and healing.

An echo implies that something is missing...

1
BILL'S DAUGHTER
Soundtrack: "Start a War" – the National

"I have to remind myself you're Bill's daughter."

His words stunned. My blood turned to acid, my body froze as if winter had suddenly descended upon my limbs. Unprotected, the force of his words bounced back and forth like an icy echo.

Bill. My father. We hadn't spoken in twenty years.

Over and over again the sentence swirled and danced, growing thicker and louder with each inhalation, threatening to swallow me whole. My husband had never met Bill, but his piercing words were aimed with crystal-clear intention. They came out of nowhere and shattered the silence, shattered my heart.

Bill's daughter. I don't even know what that means.

With those words he turned and walked away,

leaving me alone in the foreign space. We had recently sold our home of ten years, moved into a rental that was nice, but still, not home. Not yet comforting. As I stood in the kitchen, frozen with disbelief, heart pounding, my eyes darted to the familiar—the dishes in the sink, the photographs on the fridge, the spices on the rack, the shoes on my feet. I stared at the unfamiliar kitchen floor in the new apartment, stunned into silence. Silence, often followed by a sudden epiphany, has always been my default setting, my coping method.

Perhaps these severe words, this unforgiving explanation of me, were retaliation for my childish antics earlier, in the therapist's room. I had grown tired of talking in circles, analyzing personalities, hunting for reasons. Searching for solutions, like so many needles in haystacks. Working it out. So I'd fallen silent, and then ended our session by dramatically throwing my hands in the air and declaring, "Marriages fail every day. I'm done. Done."

That was too much for my husband to hear; he loathed that word. "Done" meant something was unfixable. He preferred to say, "You can't un-crack an egg." The egg might be cracked, but you can still make something of it. This was usually true. But now we were the egg, already scrambled.

At our marriage counseling session just hours ago, our therapist talked to us about our different personalities, using a new-age tool called the Enneagram to help us learn how to communicate and understand each other better. It wasn't working.

According to the Enneagram, I was a Dreamer, my husband a Fixer. The Dreamer and The Fixer. Fixer had once described us as the flag and the flag-pole. Pretty much the same thing.

Fixer is calm. He is neat, organized and hardworking. He never raises his voice, loses his temper, or speaks before thinking. He can fix anything broken or malfunctioning around the house. He can fix people, too. He's the kind of guy you can go to with an issue or problem, and in a calm and thoughtful manner, he will offer various solutions.

When we met, I was twenty-five, a young single mother with a two-year old son and a six-month starter marriage under my belt. I was in dire need of repair. My home had been turned upside down; he gave me a new, beautiful one. My son needed a father, he— without hesitation—became one. My heart, bruised and broken, longed for normalcy, stability and love. He gave me all of these things. We had a son together. We got a dog. I quit my job as a hairstylist to stay home with our children. But it was my needs, and his desire— his *need*—to fulfill them, that ultimately led to our undoing. He worked hard as a real-estate investor, putting in grueling twelve-hour plusdays to provide everything we considered necessary. And in turn, I became completely absorbed in the role of "perfect" wife and mommy.

Our therapist was taken aback when we told her that during nine years of marriage, we hadn't had a single argument. Not one. Apparently, that's not a good thing.

Our disconnection was a slow process. Like tectonic plates, we couldn't feel or see the shift. We would go days without talking beyond courtesies; weeks, then eventually months without making love. We were both guilty of nurturing everything except each other. In my dreams, we were often treading water. When we had to sell our home due to the economic recession and our enormous amount of personal debt, that's when the earthquake hit. All that we had worked so hard to secure began slipping away.

I tried to remain cheerful. Tried to stay strong. Played along, crying only when I was alone. Our mantra was "new beginnings." That had been my idea: to name the transition, give it meaning. But no one seemed truly happy. When the dog died, I saw it as an omen.

We talked to our therapist about our strained home life. The loss of control, our struggles adjusting. And then, of course, there was the other topic: emotional affairs.

In the midst of the move, lingering nervous breakdown and subsequent marriage disintegration, I had by chance reconnected with a childhood friend. A few months ago, while I was in Louisville visiting family, we had met for dinner. Our significant others were supposed to join, but Fixer stayed back in Ohio to work, and Kentucky's girlfriend had other plans, so we dined alone. I laughed like I hadn't in years, caught a wicked buzz off two IPA's, and struggled to understand half of what Kentucky said because I no longer spoke twang. As he drove me back to my aunt's home, we sang Prince songs at the top of our lungs, like we did when we were ten. I didn't want to get out of the car when our evening ended. I woke up at four the next morning, and the room wasn't the only thing spinning.

After that we talked a few times a week—emails mostly. But in my mind, we talked a hundred times a day. I didn't see the harm in my connection to

Kentucky. After all, I had known him since fifth grade. Our therapist suggested that the Dreamer in me appreciated—no, needed— the connection. Apparently, Dreamers have a hard time with loss and abandonment in the present—we long for the past and search for the future. Fleeting moments, conversations, coincidences all must mean something. When life spirals out of control, we become even more emotionally attached to people and places and ideas—fantasizing about what was and what could be. Kentucky was like finding an old journal in the rubble, battered but precious. A connection to a part of me I'd long since forgotten but had always longed for; a safe place. We talked politics, music, religion, philosophy, literature, time travel, food. We sent each other songs to listen to, recommended books to read. When he told me his biological father had left when he was a baby, and that the man I always believed to be his dad was technically not his father, I was shocked. Unlike me, he had no memories of his father, did not even know his name. Like me, he longed to know how this absence shaped him. Through our conversations I was not only getting reacquainted with him, but also getting reacquainted with me. Fixer thought we were having an affair—an 'affair of the heart.' And this angered him. Anger—an emotion that defeated him every time, only this time he'd let it show. Perhaps the counseling was working somewhat after all.

I have to remind myself you're Bill's daughter. This statement, in its purest form, was his way of saying I'm an asshole. By birth.

The truth is, I know very little about my father. Just scattered memories, fragmented observations, and assumptions gathered in a void. My mother never uttered a bad word about him. Whenever his name would come up, she'd only say, "I loved your father more than anything." My younger sister, Twig, called Bill from time to time. She sent him Christmas cards and pictures. But I hung back, and Bill never tried to reach me, though he lived less than an hour away.

Bill's daughter. I understood what Fixer meant. He blamed me, specifically some genetic predisposition—much like a disease—for the collapse of our marriage. Genetics and broken eggs. Things you cannot easily fix.

That was in January.
By March, we had separated.
In June, I called my dad.

2
FATHER'S DAY
Soundtrack : "Time of the Season" - the Zombies

He picks up after one ring, maybe half. As if he's
expecting a call. A cheerful, "Hi there!" God forbid he
say hello like everyone else.

"What the hell, you sitting there waiting for me to
call or something?" God forbid I respond with "Hey"
like everyone else.

He laughs. "Hey Twig."

Twig, my sister's nickname.

"Dad, it's Carrie."

"Oh, hey. Care. Say, uh...you wanna hang up and
start the call over again or something, act all surprised
and jovial and I'll get your name right this time?
Whaddaya say?"

"No, it's cool." I like this better. Neither of us
mentions the fact it's been twenty years since we've
talked.

"Thought it was Twig, she calls from time to time."

"I know."

"So, what'cha been up to, Care?"

"Nothing much. It's summer, the kids and I spend a lot of time at the pool. I'm working a few days a week. Mostly fun stuff."

Nothing much? Fun stuff? Such a lie. I know I'm avoiding the fact that I don't know how to answer this question. I don't know how to talk to him. I don't know how to say, "I want to know what being your daughter means, that's why I'm calling." In the background, I hear his lighter click. A Zippo. It clicks up and clicks down, always has, always will. Click. Snap.

"How are you?"

He inhales, pauses, exhales. "I used to spend so much time at the pool. You can thank me for that skin tone of yours, you know." Another inhale. "And my mom's getting crazier and crazier every day, I need to find her a place to live." Another exhale. "It's getting rough. Your mom's mom, she's what, eighty somethin' and she still does fine, right?" I know, through Twig, that my father lives with his mom, who has Alzheimer's.

"Yeah, Mammaw? She does fine, but she also exercises every day, writes crossword puzzles for a living and doesn't have Alzheimer's like your mom does," I explain.

"Yeah Twig, well my mom, all she does is walk from the fuckin' chair to the cookies then back to the chair again. That's her exercise. And she watches golf, she could watch that shit all day, loves it cuz it's green and has water and stuff."

I can't help it, I laugh uncomfortably, not that he

could tell the difference. Our ability to jump into light chit-chat confuses me. I ask how he is and he talks of golf and cookies, keeps calling me Twig. I wonder if Alzheimer's is contagious. I realize I'm pacing.

"Hey, your sister sent me a DVD, from your 50th birthday party. I can't get it to play on my DVD player."

"I'm thirty-five. It was my thirty-fifth birthday." I knew my sister had sent him the DVD; she'd asked if I was okay with her sending it. I didn't mind, although the DVD—with its photo stream documenting my life from birth to the present moment, backed up by music to tie together all the memories—seemed more appropriate for my funeral.

"Well, Care, feels like fifty to me, honey."

"I believe it," I say. This elicits an uncomfortable little laugh, from him this time.

"Did I tell you about the alien baby, Care? The one growing inside my body. I can feel him moving around in there. And I need another root canal, lost another filling, and I saw some commercial for prostate issues and I think I need that medicine."

"Don't buy that commercial bullshit, they just want to sell you drugs. You want to tell me more about this alien baby?" I assumed he was sick, and the alien baby must be a metaphor for cancer or something. Twig had mentioned he wasn't well, but that he wouldn't elaborate, wouldn't seek treatment.

"Aw hell, I don't want to talk about that right now, but the tooth thing has me really angry, limits my food options. Suppose I'll eat Salisbury steak again tonight, that's always good in a pinch, isn't it honey?"

He calls me honey, like we speak daily. He's

deeply disappointed to hear that I don't eat Salisbury steak, that the only time I ever ate it was with him, twice maybe. This doesn't stop him from telling me in great detail the specifics of his Salisbury steak recipe. More small talk, more bullshit, the language he knows best.

"God, they're good even cold, Twig, get 'em out of the fridge around 2 AM. Mmm Mmm. But enough of that, I was about to watch a movie, some flop with Renee Zellweger in it. Did some laundry today, baked some cookies, that's my life, what's up with you?"

"Nothing, really".

What is wrong with me? My husband has moved out, I'm searching... what do you say when someone asks you to tell them about your life? Rarely the truth, unless you're paying them, like a therapist. Even then, sometimes you lie. But I can small talk with the best of them, like Bill. As a hairstylist, I talk to people all day, following their conversational lead. Sometimes it's deep, sometimes it's superficial. Bill's surfing. I'm wading.

"So, how's life in meth country?" He lives in Blanchester, Ohio, approximately 45 minutes away.

"Well, did I tell you June has cancer?" I tell him no, I didn't know that. How would I know anything about Bill's sister-in-law? "Yeah, as I sit here smoking a cigarette. She has lung cancer. She's a hurtin' cowgirl right now, chemo and radiation, hair fallin' out. It's not all bad news, though. I think it can be cured."*Oh,really.*

"Yep, June has cancer, Sharon needs a kidney, I don't know how the hell Mike is, we haven't talked in a year, and you know my brother Danny in Texas, I do wonder how he's doin, haven't talked to him in like fifteen years, heard he had a stroke awhile ago, could be dead for all I know. Family. Yep, we're a close family."

The names are familiar to me. They are his brothers and sisters, the aunts and uncles I wouldn't recognize on the street. He erupts into a violent cough that makes me stop pacing and pull the phone away from my ear.

"Hell, Care, there's got to be some good news. Oh I know, they're about to elect another Pork Queen soon," he says with a laugh, still laced with the guts of that dreadful cough. Pork Queen. Pork. It goes from squealing pig to ground meat in less than thirty seconds, and then we eat it.

I sense by his jokes that he hates his life in Blanchester, relies on harsh wit to get him though. His wit, and today, Renee Zellweger's squint.

"Yeah, I'll get through this, I'll get rid of this baby. It's pretty fucking hard to knock me down. You get that from me, too. Now, poke me in the eye I'll cry like a baby. Stab me with a pencil in the arm, that hurts too. Hey, maybe that pencil lead in my arm is why my fillings keep falling out. Lead poisoning finally workin its way up to my teeth. Next it's my brain."

"That's not pencil lead in your arm. It's a blue mole, I have one too. It's called a Blue Nevis." We have the same mole on our left forearm. The doctor told me it's hereditary. I am back to pacing.

"No kidding. I always wondered who stabbed me? Blue mole. Huh."

"Sorry about your teeth and stuff, Dad… but I want to know what's up with this alien baby? Seriously."

"Yeah right… me too… you know, seriously, humans should have evolved by now to have shark teeth. One falls out and immediately is replaced with another one. Why can't we do that? Course now with the oil spill, who wants to be a fuckin' shark? All kiddin' aside Twig, we should have every skimmer available out there cleaning that shit up. Hell, I know I'm not President, but that's what I'd do. All those fish swimming in that crap. Next year I'll run for President, why not, course the baby might be born by then. My only concern is where's the alien baby gonna come out? I might wish it'd come out just like it does in the movie."

He hears me start to laugh again, he's reeling me in, feels his grandiose charm working and says, "Yeah, I haven't changed a bit. Enough about me, what's goin on with you? Seriously. Let's get serious."

He keeps calling me Twig, making it hard to take him seriously, so I tell him, "Well, I went to Lexington last night to visit some friends, that was fun." Now I'm surfing.

"Why Lexington?"

"Dad, I used to live there, in sixth grade."

"Oh yeah, alright, so hey, why won't this DVD work in my player, the one from your 50th birthday?"

I wish I could tell him I think it's sweet that he keeps trying to watch the video my mom made for my birthday. I also want to ask if he's curious to see all he missed, but I don't. That's too deep, we've got to stay at the surface. So instead I ask, "Have you tried watching it on a computer?"

"Honey, my computer's so goddamn old the number keys are Roman numerals. Maybe I should try it at the library computer, when I turn Renee Zellweger in for Nicole Kidman. And don't tell me you don't like

Nicole Kidman, I don't want to hear it, I love that movie Dead Calm, you're losing my favor now if you tell me you don't like her, I have all of her movies."

Dead. Calm. Have I ever had favor?

I tell him I'll check her movies out and revisit my feelings for Nicole Kidman, that I do love Moulin Rouge, does that help? I tell him I've called him Dad more times today than I'm comfortable with, that the entire conversation's been bullshit, and I'd like to know more about the alien baby, to which he laughs and says, "You know Care, I always did love tall redheads." He's still thinking about Nicole Kidman.

"You married two blondes."

He replies, "Yeah, I guess. And you're wrong, I married three."

His laugh over three failed marriages leads to the next subject. "Your sister tells me she found some pictures of me, from when I was a young man, in a sailor suit. She said she'd mail them to me but never did. That, or they've just stopped delivering the mail here in Blanchester. I mean, that's totally possible." Click. Snap. Inhale.

"I haven't seen the pictures; I don't know where they are. Why were you in a sailor suit? Was it Halloween or something?"

"No, it's from high school, musical theater stuff." Exhale.

"You were in musical theater?" I hate musicals.

"Yes, you didn't know? I got a full scholarship to University of Cincinnati's College-Conservatory of Music, for singing and dancing. I could sing and dance my way through anything."

I had no idea. I'm not surprised, for here he is, here

we are, singing and dancing our way through this conversation. I stop pacing my living room, sit down, and cradle the phone between my ear and shoulder. I prop my feet up and surrender to the show. His voice sounds exactly the way I remember. A song and dance man. I resign to let him keep dancing.

"So what happened? Did you go?"

"Well Care, I did, and then I had to take ballet. Two thirds of the class was guys who talked funny and acted funny, and I thought hell no you're not seeing old Bill out there doin' ballet. I could have been a movie star. Jesus Carrie, what else you don't know about me?"

He pauses to re-light his smoke. Click. Snap. I wonder if he's pacing or sitting. I wonder what his house looks like. "Did you know I was going to be a cop? Passed the training and exam with flying colors, but then they gave me a lie detector test and I failed it. Those sons of bitches do work, apparently. Oh well, glad that career didn't work out, Twig, shit, Care. I tell you what, I'm disappointed you don't know these things, why don't you make a list, all the things you want to know, I'll tell ya. Brutal honesty, ask me anything. Do it now, before the alien baby is born. You know, in case I don't survive the birth."

"Really, brutal honesty? You just told me you failed a lie detector test."

I can practically hear him shrug. "Why would I lie? You've got nothing invested in me and I got nothing to lose." Now we're getting somewhere. I sit forward, anticipating, ready, breathing... He exhales and interrupts my thoughts with, "You still collecting vinyl records? Twig mentioned you do."

"I do, I am." I lean back again, "Nothing like you,

I'm sure. I remember you had quite a collection."

"That's a good idea, vinyl's a dying glory. You get your love of music from me, you know. Have you seen my new turntable? It's beautiful, gold plated, pendulum arm rests in this fluid, it moves not only up and down but left and right, you see, follows the grooves... they only made 1,000 turntables like mine. Have to sell mine though, pay for this tooth and the alien baby, such a shame. You'd hear the difference, though. I used to have hundreds of albums, you know, I had them all. I hate to have to sell the thing."

I'm taking it all in, following his grooves up and down and left and right, sitting, listening, pacing, and responding.

"That sucks you have to sell it. People like us can hear the difference, someone will buy it." I realize I've never said 'people like us' to him before, but of course I'm only referring to our shared love of music. "It sounds cool. If I had the money, I'd buy it from you in a heartbeat."

"If I had the money, I might give it to you. You see, the alien does ache a lot, and my tooth, I'm so damn tired of thinking 'what can I front chew today?' I can only use my front teeth, ya see. I think about what's for dinner and think, 'yeah, that's a front chew, what can I front fucking chew today?' The saddest thing is, I can't put onions on my chili anymore. You ever try to front chew an onion the size of half a pea? I do enjoy chewing my food. My whole world's falling apart, and now no more onions on my chili."

"You need to take care of this alien baby."

"Don't forget the teeth. First the teeth, I'm hungry. Hey, let's eat guacamole together sometime."

I sit forward again, and exclaim, "Oh my God, I love guacamole! You like guacamole?" I can't hide my excitement over this seemingly small thing we might have in common.

"Well, no, I've never actually had it, but it seems like a front chew. I gotta expand my list of choices." I lean back, exhausted, confused. All the singing and dancing has me whirling.

"Alright, Dad, I gotta go. Do you have my phone number?"

"No, what is it? I'll write it down on my grocery list here, under steak, bread and peanut butter. You mind being under the peanut butter?"

"No, I don't mind being under the peanut butter."

After our conversation, I feel like I'm beneath the peanut butter already, ground up like pork, pureed like guacamole. I give him my number and envision his list—bread, steak, peanut butter, Care's number. I think if you're on a grocery list you're doomed to one of two fates: you're either going to be eaten, or thrown away.

I'm chewing my nails and visualizing myself as various food products when he interrupts my thoughts once again.

"Thanks for calling Care, it's been a really long time, I really do appreciate it. And see, I got your name right this time."

"Alright, talk soon. Call me. And, by the way, you know it's Fathers Day, right? So, you know, Happy Fathers Day."

3
MARTINIS WITH JESUS
Soundtrack : "Don't Cross the River" - the Association

I always knew when it was Sunday. My favorite day. I counted down the days, hours, minutes, then suffered patiently through the hymnals and prayers at church, knowing afterwards we would go spend the day with our dad. Sunday was 'visitation day.' My mother was always extra chatty during the drive to Dad's, chalking it up to her nerves 'or something.' She talked non-stop as I counted stop signs, traffic lights, trees.

It was 1980 and my parents had divorced.

I could feel my Mom's heart breaking a little bit more every time we turned down his driveway. I might have heard it too, if it weren't for her constant chatter. His home was an oasis for me. In a stark departure from our duplex surrounded by dirt, he lived in a giant house with a pool, a dog, and his girlfriend. Her name was Debi, with an *i*, which I thought was very cool. I wished my name was spelled Ker*i*.

I was born in Cincinnati, but we moved to Texas when I was four or five. Debi, as it turns out, was the reason for that move. Sure, my dad had received a promotion, but the real bonus was that his girlfriend was moving to Texas, too. When my mom found out, she'd packed us up and driven us to Kentucky to live with her parents. My dad begged for her to return, and of course she did, desperately wanting to believe that Debi was history and they could begin again. He tried, and failed, to live a double life. My mom stayed in Texas anyway, likely too exhausted to move again. She also wanted us to have a relationship with our dad—generous, considering the circumstances.

Despite his philandering, she still loved him. Driving to his house, Mom would check herself in the rearview mirror repeatedly, smoothing a stray hair, examining her teeth. She wanted to look her best for him. I felt guilty that his house was my favorite place. He let us swim for hours, eat whatever we wanted (there was always plenty, unlike home), and music played continuously throughout the house, even out by the pool. Always there was music. And now, always Debi, with her adopted Texas accent, big blonde hair, and giant eyelashes. She called me "Darlin'. I loved that, too.

Dad would answer the door in his swim trunks: 1970's style, too short, royal blue with white trim. My mother would glance inside, perhaps looking for the woman who'd stolen her husband. We'd kiss her goodbye and make a mad dash for the bathroom, to shed our church clothes and pull on our swimsuits. That time after church was sacred; we had just one day a week with him.

I remember the Sunday we rang the doorbell, and waited. We rang it again and again, so many times I lost count. I can still hear that doorbell today, can still feel the pressure on my fingertip.

All was quiet except for the sound of the door chime echoing in the empty house.

He never answered.

That didn't stop us from looking. We walked around the sprawling ranch, peeked in the windows and through the wooden slats of the privacy fence. No furniture, no music, no dog barking, no Debi.

We drove home in silence.

I still recall the dream I had that night, as raw and vivid as it was thirty years ago.

I'm swimming in the pool, and I'm so proud—it's the deep end and I'm in there all by myself. There's my Dad, sitting on the pool deck, martini in one hand, cigarette in the other. He's laughing and smiling towards me, and right beside him is Jesus. Jesus Christ is hanging out by the pool, and he's drinking a martini, too! I'm doing back flips, over and over again, showing off for the two men. I don't need to hold my nose underwater. I keep popping up after each rotation, making sure both Jesus and my father are watching. They laugh as I splash wildly. I can hear their laughter underwater. They raise their cocktail glasses and cheer as I pop up for air. I can hear the music blasting, see the dog pacing, she's worried I may drown. I jump out and climb the steps to the diving board, hover at the end, bouncing, courageous enough to leap, again no need to hold my nose, for I am not afraid. I touch the bottom of the pool, tap the drain with a toe, and push up from beneath the water to find an empty pool deck. The dog, my dad, the music, Jesus... all gone. Treading water, spinning, panicking... I'm not supposed to be in the pool alone. From behind I hear a buzzing sound. My bouncing on the board has disturbed a bees' nest that lay concealed beneath the diving stand. They are flying towards me, angry and humming. I slip back underwater, eyes open, nose held tightly closed.

I woke, face wet with tears.
He never answered.

4
NEW BEGINNINGS
Soundtrack: "Apartment Story" – the National

Three days later, I call Bill again.

"Hi!" Apparently, this is how he always answers the phone. Jazz hands, song and dance style.

"Hey, it's Carrie."

"Wow, two calls in twenty years, what's the occasion?"

I bite my lip in restraint.

"Well, I've been thinking. I'd like to come visit you. Take you up on your offer to talk about some things. Do you remember saying that, or were you kidding?"

"No, nuh-uh baby, I remember. I'd love to sit down and talk to ya'." Click. Snap.

"Ok, well, how about next Sunday? And, I've also been thinking I'd like to buy your turntable."

"Oh Care, you don't have to do that." He sounds

surprised, yet sad.

"I know I don't have to. I actually need a new turntable, mine's pretty beat up, and you're going to sell it anyway, so if I can afford it, I'd like to buy it from you."

"Have you even seen this thing, what you're buying?"

"I looked it up online, I know what it is." I'd researched it, along with how to help your children cope with divorce, emotional affairs, and various genetic personality theories. I'd even Googled "Am I an asshole because my father is?" I didn't want to think about divorce, genetic theories and 'affairs of the heart' made my head spin, but the turntable, that I could grasp. It's a Reference Hydraulic Transcription, by J.A. Michell. It's gorgeous. Looks like a spacecraft, or a piece of art. You can find it in the movie A Clockwork Orange and 2001 A Space Odyssey. Apparently, Kubrick was a fan. Yep, that I can deal with. And I can't let him sell it to anyone else.

"Okay, so Sunday, you'll be here Sunday. Do you know where I live?"

"No, what's your address? I'll put it under the peanut butter." He laughs, and then coughs, spastically. We both grow silent, and I ask if that was the alien baby.

"Yeah, I'm not feeling so hot—alien, tooth, everything. I've been up and down all week. It's getting worse."

"Where does it hurt?"

"Inside my ribcage, up and down, boob to stomach. I'm pregnant I tell ya'. Constant sharp pain. Alien hell. I take ibuprofen, probably too many, doubt it's healthy.

I bear with it, breathe through it. I can't lay down most of the time so I just sleep in the chair."

It does, in fact, sound a lot like pregnancy. "What are you going to do about it?"

"Nothin. I need some money."

No one ever thinks they are financially prepared for the baby, real or alien. I know he needs money, that's the other reason I'm buying the turntable; like some twisted backwards baby shower, a sepia-tinged scene from a Tim Burton movie.

"Well, think about your price for the turntable. I'll be there Sunday, with money, if you decide to sell it to me. That could be a start. Sunday morning. I'll call when I'm on my way. Cool?"

"That'd be great, Care. Maybe we can hang out, watch a movie."

Rolling my eyes, I sigh, "I sincerely want to talk to you. Were you serious about talking to me? You know, real talking? No more singing and dancing?"

He pauses. Inhale. Exhale. Finally, he sounds genuine. "Yes, Care, real talking. Sounds good. See you Sunday."

Real talking, with my father. Something we've avoided for two decades. Have I avoided him, or has he avoided me? Or are we so alike that we avoid each other naturally, like magnets reversed? Sitting on the couch in the quiet unfamiliar apartment, clinging to the phone and staring at the ceiling, I am so alone I don't even want to push 'end' on the phone.

The boys are with Fixer for most of the weekend, and I don't know what to do with myself. I am thankful to be working more again; work distracts me, keeps me busy. I need my job as a hairstylist—not just the money, but also the fuel of the people and their energy. Work absorbs two days of my weekend alone, Friday and Saturday. Lately I've been meeting friends out for dinner, drinks, or both. I've told a few of them about the separation—most were as shocked as my family. My friend, Shakespeare, is particularly intrigued and sympathetic. He's an actor, which means he loves a good tragedy. Since the separation he's invited me to parties and outings, plays and movies. I enjoy his company, though I think he invites me because he feels sorry for me, which is fine. Better him than me. Sometimes we sit on his back deck and he asks a million questions about my family and my children and my feelings. I prefer to look at the stars and identify the constellations, but I answer his questions and let him refill my wine when it's empty.

Sundays, sans work and social obligations, are the hardest. I wish I still had my dog to walk with while I wait for the boys to get home. For twelve years, I've been the one to tuck them in every night, to wake up with them every morning. Now I have three long, eerily quiet nights without them. I make sure to practice yoga during this time, because it helps me relax; clears my head. But despite the yoga, and knowing better, if I'm alone, I often sit and listen to melancholy music, think too much and drink too much wine. Frantically trying to fill the void and defuse the quiet in this unfamiliar space without my children. Easily the hardest part of my day.

I miss my old house. It was the only true home I've ever had, and certainly the longest. Having a stable home, one that I owned and nurtured and loved, a place where I could raise my boys and create memories. It had meant more than I cared to admit. When I think about our old house now, the tears flow of their own accord. And in my dreams, I'm still there, but the house is often flooded and I'm swimming around trying to save something, anything.

I wonder if my children are sad too, despite how hard they try to imitate our feigned optimism about the future. To embrace the "new beginnings." How could they not be sad? I know what it feels like to leave a home you love. I moved so often as a child—from house to house, duplex to apartment, city to city. I never wanted that for them. I wanted stability. I wanted perfection.

But I'm starting to realize perfection doesn't exist. That I can't always control circumstances. That even when everything looks flawless—*especially* when it looks flawless—it's not. That's what upsets my friends and family the most. Fixer and I appeared to have it all together.

I miss watching the boys sleep. Over the years, I thought about Bill while watching them dream. I'd wonder how he could have missed so many moments like that, the simple, peaceful beauty of a sleeping child. When my children were infants, I'd hold them the entire time they napped, content to feel and hear every breath. I'd put my nose right next to their lips and inhale as they exhaled. I thought about Bill sometimes then, too, wondering how he could not see, hear, or hold the very humans he helped bring into this world. Not smell their breath or their hair.

I don't think it's a coincidence that a baby's first word is usually "Dada." True, it may be the easiest thing to say, but perhaps there's a reason for that. It must be hard to be a dad. During pregnancy, when the mom carries the child a bond is formed immediately. She goes through the stages of growth with her baby, and during birth feels just how painful love can be. She's the first to hold him, she nurses him, and knows intuitively what he needs. How can a father ever comprehend or replicate that bond? He can't. So the baby says Dada first to send a message: I need you, too.

All my life, I've wanted to know why he left us. Why he wasn't there, never answered the door. I intend to ask him these things.

My current state of isolation is different than before. Before our separation, I wondered if it was normal for a married woman to feel alone. Now I don't know what "normal" means. Does anybody? Fixer and I have stopped going to counseling. Instead, we meet for lunch once or twice a week. Our lunches are good; productive. Hindsight is providing clarity. It seems by separating, we have been able to break down our disconnection. When did it begin? Was it the suburban role-playing, the financial strain, the gradual decline in communication and lovemaking? How can we stop it? Should we try? Is it possible to start over—to claim a new beginning?

Sometimes we take walks together. It is during one of these walks that he brings up the idea of having an open marriage. We had talked about it before, in jest. I'd joked that it sounded like a good idea, would certainly have worked for my father. I guess Fixer thought I'd been serious. Fixers need to give, to find solutions—and often sacrifice themselves to please others.

Fixer wants to stay married, and believes that incorporating an open marriage will enable me to fill some kind of void. He thinks my emotional attachment to Kentucky is a sign that I need more, something he can't give me. It's not his first choice, but he's trying to stay open and flexible. He was reassuring me he would never leave. That he was committed to finding a solution.

"Solution" has many definitions. It can be an answer to a problem, or it can be an ending.

Part of me is intrigued, wondering if this could work. People change, desires come and go, and marriage is strange. What if you're free to follow these desires, in an open and honest way? How would that feel? Is that what I want? The other part of me believes if you were going to have an open relationship, it should be clarified before you commit. Post-commitment, it seems ill-fitting. Like a band-aid applied to wet skin: it's not gonna stick. I never mention it to Kentucky, because he's part of the reason Fixer thinks we need an open marriage. I can't saddle him with that, can't have him feeling he's responsible for any part of this.

Fixer and I walk and talk often, neither of us wearing our wedding rings. Our conversations, though heavy in subject matter, are starting to feel relaxed and free. In a strange and surprising way, we both seem happier. And though I miss the boys' constant presence, when I observe them now, I see they enjoy spending time with their dad. They are getting to know him better. Their relationship with him is blossoming. And Fixer loves being with them more. During lunch one day, he confessed he'd previously been phoning in the role of Dad: working too much, missing lots of little things. I sense he is blossoming, too.

I realize I'm jealous.

I want to blossom. I want to know my own dad. My head and heart swirl with questions—who am I? Where have I come from, what role has Bill played in who I've become? I fear I've lived my life in a reactionary state, answering to his absence. I'm afraid I am just like Bill, incapable of solid relationships. With the exception of my two children, I've perfected the art of numbing my true feelings, building walls, keeping most people at just the right distance. Like Bill?

And with the boys, I'll admit I am the definition of a helicopter parent. I loved my job, but quit working full-time to stay home when each was born. I couldn't handle the guilt of not being there for them every waking moment. When they were babies, they slept right beside me, the idea of them sleeping in a separate room terrifying and incomprehensible. What if there was a fire and I couldn't get to them? What if they cried for me and I couldn't hear them? These thoughts paralyzed me with fear. I nursed as long as they let me, whenever they wanted to, because not only was it the best food I could give, but it was a bond no one else could offer. I never hired a babysitter, ever. I went along on every field trip, was the room mother when they were in preschool and elementary school. When it became clear that my youngest son needed specialized schooling that we could not afford, I decided to homeschool him. When my oldest son asked if he could join us at home, I let him. I built a classroom into our basement, joined every homeschooling group in our city, researched every method, sought unique experiences and educational opportunities, spent an unbelievable amount of money on textbooks, field trips, art supplies, and tutors. Six months into our first homeschooling year, I had an emotional breakdown, terrified that I wouldn't be able to educate them properly or get them into the best colleges. Responding to my extreme stress, my neighbors and family brought me flowers and casseroles, like someone had died. Someone was dying. Me.

The boys are still homeschooled, though now I rely heavily on classes taught through a co-op we can barely afford. Their grandparents help with tuition. The boys love it, so I'm happy—broke and indebted to the hierarchy, but happy.

I know my parenting style is unhealthy, and unsustainable—a reaction to my own childhood and Bill's absence, certainly. And I'm beginning to realize that while my actions have shown them I will always be there for them, they have also worked to guarantee my children will always need me. How can we ever find the balance?

I have to remind myself you're Bill's daughter. Shortly after moving out, Fixer apologized for those words. He'd said it out of anger, to hurt me. I have no idea what it means. I am scared, yet curious. Fixer's words haunt and propel me, and a little alien baby is telling me to hurry.

5
THE TURNTABLE
Soundtrack: "Hallelujah" – k.d. lang

The following Sunday, I wake up early. Fortified by an entire pot of coffee, I call Bill, as promised. I am afraid he will cancel on me, but I'm even more afraid of arriving without calling. What if he isn't there? The unanswered doorbell still echoes in my head.

He does answer, and doesn't cancel our plans. I leave right away. I am too nervous to eat, hyped up on caffeine, windblown from the 45-minute drive, shaking and buzzed and starved in every way by the time I arrive.

He is waiting outside for me, sitting in a white plastic chair. I look around as I park my Volvo, trying to take it all in without judging, avoid looking directly at him. I have imagined this moment over and over, and the reality of it is surreal. After all these years, I have made the pilgrimage to Bill's. Alone.

His home is in a trailer park, tucked behind an abandoned ceramics factory. On his neighbor's porch is a rusted baby swing. Another neighbor has stuck plastic flowers in the dirt of the trailer's window boxes, even though it is summer and real flowers could survive. Another neighbor's minivan has the words "Kickin', Punchin' and Still Married! Happy Anniversary!" scrawled across the back window. Down the street, pink balloons wave from a flag pole, welcoming home a baby girl. My father's trailer is weathered and pale gray. There is no adornment in his yard, just an old white Lincoln Town Car parked out front. The car is covered in dirt and pollen, like it hasn't moved in years.

Though it is only 9:30 in the morning, I feel wasted and exhausted. My hands shake as I roll up my car window, open the door and step outside to find him walking toward me. My blood returns to acid, my body freezes once again.

To say we resemble each other would be like saying Michael Douglas looks a little like Kirk, or that the Olsen twins share some similarities. I am Bill's daughter, at least physically, on every level possible. His eyes, large and almond shaped, almost but not quite black. His shoulders broad, his posture perfect, his presence strong. His hair, once dark like mine, is now the color of dirty snow, yellow tinged and ashy. He's wearing faded jeans and a short sleeved white button down shirt. White sneakers, too clean to have been worn for anything industrious, peek from beneath the hem of his jeans.

He's dressed like the lead singer of the Moody Blues. Dated, but clean. His shirt pocket bulges with a pack of cigarettes—an unfamiliar logo, no longer Marlboros—along with his trusty Zippo.

He smells familiar, and I'm surprised by the comfort the scent brings. As he hugs me, I inhale my earliest childhood memories. The happy ones. I am taken aback by how natural the embrace feels, yet still I hug him back cautiously. He repeats my name, "Carrie, Carrie, Carrie" in his deep baritone. He could have been a movie star, his voice that of a leading man. I say nothing. I have never allowed myself to practice this feeling. I am ill-prepared, and silent.

He pulls back, looks at me and laughs, and then pulls me back in for another embrace, still repeating my name. I am skin and bones in his arms, the stress of the past few months eating away at my already slight frame. He asks if I am hungry.

"I am. I'm starving, actually."

"Alright then, let's go inside and eat something. Your grandmother's inside, too. Do you remember her? Because she won't remember you." He laughs at his own joke as I follow him up the splitting wooden steps. There are four, I count them. Four steps, one deep breath, and I am inside his home.

There's the odor of stale cigarettes. Strange how that smell can sometimes make me smile. His various houses were always immaculate, yet the aroma of just-smoked cigarettes forever lingered. The furniture in his trailer is dated, worn but cozy. The art on the walls is generic and cheap, the kind of mass-produced landscapes and flower pastels you might find in motel rooms throughout the country. He catches me staring at a baby doll head, edged with a doily, hanging on the kitchen wall. "Your grandma made that." No other explanation necessary.

I look at his mother, resting in a wingback chair, thin and frail and melting. She looks nothing like I remember. Her name is Dorothy and she was once so thick and robust, so loud and (kindly) domineering. She gazes at me, the stranger in her home, and smiles. Her dentures slip from her mouth, prompting her to exclaim, "Bill, I think I need some new teeth!"

"Mom, this is my daughter Carrie." He yells this truth to her, then mumbles something to me about not taking it personally that he had to explain my identity. I'm actually relieved that she doesn't remember me, because if she did it would force us to face reality. But in the next breath, I'm saddened by the fact that my grandmother has no idea who I am, and that I never really knew her or my dad growing up. Staring at the two of them, fearing I might cry, I glance toward the door and contemplate a quick get-away.

Dorothy's perky voice thwarts my plans. "It sure is nice to meet you!" Again, her teeth slip. My eyes dart to the doily-framed doll head effigy and then back at my grandmother's hopeful, almost childlike face.

"Mom," Bill shouts, "I'm going to make some eggs. You want some eggs for breakfast?" She shakes her head 'no', tired of her teeth slipping. Her eyes are fixed on the television, which appears to be showing either the news or some celebrity interview. Either way, it's foreign to me: I don't really watch TV.

He doesn't ask if I like eggs or not, just cooks me two over easy, fluid and runny, just how I like them. He serves them with a side of sausage and piece of toast. Simple food, like he cooked for me when I was little. Perhaps he remembers. He doesn't cook anything for himself, just sits beside me, smoking and making a grocery list. I eat in silence, swirling the runny yolk with the tips of my toast. "I know you just got here Care, but I was wondering if you could take me to the grocery store?"

"Um, ok." I shrug. "Sure." I find this odd and irritating. After twenty years, the first thing he wants to do together is go grocery shopping?

"We can leave her alone for just a little bit." With his head he motions toward Dorothy. "It won't take long."

I finish my food as he scrawls his list, still taking in his space. Everything has a place; every recycled and reused container is labeled. For fun, he spells sugar 'SCHUGAR' on the vintage Tupperware. The one that holds his candy is simply labeled 'MINE,' all caps. I smile, remembering the hairbrush he kept on his bathroom counter was labeled 'MINE.' I used it anyway, because he told me not to.

On his fridge is my sister's most recent Christmas card; beside it, a picture of my family, husband included, taken two years ago in Chicago on our last family vacation. Twig must have sent it to him.

At the store, Bill gathers his essentials: bologna, eggs, cheese puffs (had to switch from Cheetos due to his damn teeth, he explains), and some beer. Cheap beer. At the checkout he orders three packs of cigarettes, just under four dollars a pack. Cheap cigarettes. He knows the cashier by name, and she knows his. In fact, everyone in the supermarket knows my dad, saying hello as they stare at me, at us, trying to make the connection. I am relieved when he makes no introductions. Some things are hard to explain, and I don't feel like making small-talk today. Unless they are all blind, they must know who I am.

Back home, we unpack his groceries together. As he reaches for a fresh cigarette, he asks, "Do you want to see the turntable? I keep it over here, so it won't get dirty." Lighting his cheap smoke with his expensive lighter—Click. Snap—he motions for me to follow. The turntable rests on top of his dryer, right outside his bedroom, covered by a towel. He lifts the towel slightly, as if the turntable is in the morgue awaiting identification. He tells me how delicate she is. The turntable is a she, he explains, because she is so complicated, so precise, so beautiful. He handles her as such. Like he is in love.

"You sure you want to sell this to me?"

"Yes, I'm sure. No, I don't really want to, but I have to. I was going to sell it on ebay anyway, so I'd rather you have it." He takes a few steps away from her, inhaling a long drag from his smoke, thinking.

"I'll sell it to you for 600 bucks."

Although his price is much higher than I expected, I agree and pull out my checkbook. He stops me and asks if I mind paying him in cash.

Back to the store we go, where I find an ATM and withdraw six hundred-dollar bills.

Back at his trailer, instead of going inside, he stops and sits in his plastic chair, pulls another one up for me. Click. Snap. We sit. It feels like rain is moving in. We sit and wait, neither of us knowing where to begin.

The silence, the pause, the tip of my finger, the edge of the diving board, the bees buzzing. I ask if I can bum a cigarette, and without hesitation he hands one to me, abolishing my eight smoke-free years. I light it—click, inhale, snap, exhale—and muster the courage to begin.

"I have this memory. Part memory, part dream. I don't know what's what..." I tell him what I remember, what happened 29 years ago in Texas, and ask him for clarity. "Is my memory true? Did you just leave?" On cue, a light mist begins falling from the sky. He answers by singing something about raindrops and his love leaving.

Then his shoulders hunch and his presence somewhat evaporates. "Well, Care, I made a lot of bad moves. And I didn't know what else to do. I left you guys in Texas because I didn't know what else to do. I thought, fuck it, I'll just leave."

Fuck it. I'll just leave.

In this moment I am six again, racing around his house, and I ache to erase this panicked memory. He watches his cigarette burn, and I watch mine. He repeats, "I didn't know what else to do."

Fuck it. I'll just leave. *Fuck it?* I am repulsed by the simplicity of his excuse.

"I left Texas, Care, because your mom was after me for child support. We went to court, she put me in jail, of course you girls had no idea. I borrowed money from friends. Paid her off. Split town. You should have anger inside of you because of what I did. I made a lot of bad moves. Did you come here to tell me you were angry?"

"No."

"I have been, basically, an asshole Carrie. Wasn't trying to be one… a jerk maybe. I uh, was always fightin' battles, didn't have time to deal with you kids and stuff. When I was away from you guys, lots of years went by that I, I can't account for."

"What battles?"

"No matter what I did, there were always battles, always a war."

We both flick our smokes toward the sky.

The rain intensifies. Bill offers to load the turntable into my car before it gets worse. He carries her, still wrapped in a towel, as if she is an infant venturing from home for the first time. I open the passenger door for him. He places her on the seat and stares tenderly, then removes some folded note paper from his back pocket.

"Care, I got a favor to ask you."

What now? I just hope we don't have to go back to the grocery.

"I've put together a list of songs I haven't heard

in a long, long time. Could you make a CD for me?" I unfold the lists, three full pages, front and back. Handwritten, specific, all caps. A quick glance over the song titles and I begin to understand. Never underestimate the power of music to say what you cannot.

"Yeah, I can do this for you. I'd be happy to. I'll give you a call, maybe bring the CD back next week?"

We hug, and as I open my car door a fresh Click. Snap. grabs my attention.

"Hey Care. At the time, I didn't know how to be married. I didn't know how to not be married. But I knew how to leave."

6
BONE COLLECTOR
Soundtrack: "Never My Love" – the Association

Shortly after my dad disappeared, we moved back
to Kentucky. It was 1981. My pappaw had gone to
be with Jesus for real, so we moved in with my
mammaw, and left Texas behind for good. My mom
promised we'd love it there. And I did. The
beautiful landscape stretched like taffy: corn,
tobacco fields, so many big and healthy trees. There
was a weeping willow in front of our new home, my
favorite type of tree to this day. The farm in
Kentucky felt warm and happy, despite the deep
sadness that clung to all the women in the tiny
house with its blue vinyl siding.

We lived on 32 acres in the middle of nowhere,
a half-hour outside of Louisville. Remote, perfect
for escaping reality. On our land was a hill, and on
that hill I found my rock, on top of the highest point

of the biggest hill overlooking my new world.

I shared a room, and a full-sized bed, with my mammaw. My mother and Twig slept in the other bedroom. Jesus hung above Mammaw and me, a constant reminder of resurrection. Adorned with palm branches and rosaries, he hovered, motionless. Twig and Mom had a still life of flowers above their bed. They seemed to sleep more peacefully.

Every night, I feverishly prayed my rosary, fully believing if I didn't, terrible things would happen. I slept adorned in miraculous medals, terrified that if I died without them around my neck, I'd be trapped in purgatory forever. But I only prayed authentically when I was alone on my rock.

My rock didn't toss and turn at night; didn't have conditions and requirements. Didn't snore or yell like my mammaw often did, as she dreamed of and talked to my pappaw in her fitful sleep.

It was the rock that healed me, grew me up and taught me to listen. On my rock, the doorbell's echo dimmed. My rock jutted out from the crest, lifting me away from the sadness and the unknowns. I believed it was placed specifically by God, in that spot, high above our tiny vinyl home, above the cornfields and the hills and the cows and the trees, just for me, for He knew I would come seeking answers. It became my quiet refuge, where I would go to sit, listen, and close my eyes to hear Him clearly. I'd open them to pray.

Driving from Texas to Kentucky is a spotty memory. My mother played many songs on our Chevette's eight-track system, one of which she played repeatedly. "Never My Love." I knew without asking that it was their song.

My parents were married on October 11th, 1969 in Cincinnati. He was nineteen, she was twenty. Before they married, they broke up. I'm not sure why. If you ask her about that time, my mother can still convey her heartbreak. My father tried for months to reach her, but her parents refused to pass along a message. They thought he was a playboy, no good for their daughter. My mother looked for him every weekend, at different bars she knew he frequented. One night, searching for my father, she had too much to drink and got into an accident driving home. The following day, her father broke down and gave her my dad's messages, to prevent her from being so foolish again. They married a few months later.

My grandparents were right about him, but my mother was deeply in love.

When I look at their wedding album or hear their song, I'm overcome with feelings of youth, happiness, sadness and love. I'm also reminded that many promises are made and then forgotten. In my favorite photo, my father is holding my mother close, cheek to cheek, hand in hand. His mouth brushing against her right ear. I like to imagine he's singing their song to her.

Outside of school, sleep, and paranoid prayer, I spent every waking moment exploring the land. It's where I came alive, unconfined. I found buried treasures in the hills. Hunted for bones. Explored every inch of wilderness, my wilderness. If it was storming, or too dark to explore, I occupied my time listening to my mother's music on my grandparents' old turntable. The selections were sparse, but decent—Kenny Rogers, Neil Diamond, Willie Nelson, Anne Murray, The Commodores, Michael Jackson and the Saturday Night Fever soundtrack. While my mom, Twig, and Mammaw watched television, I shut the door to the family room, danced and sang, still wild in nature.

On the farm, I was always a mess. My mother insisted on checking me for ticks each night before my bath. She usually found one or two burrowed in my hair. I didn't mind, as long as she pulled them off. Ticks attached themselves to the dog, too. Whiskey was my uncle's German Shepherd. My aunt, uncle, and two cousins lived down the gravel road, in the only other house we could see. As soon as we arrived on the farm, Whiskey became my honorary dog, my companion during my daily explorations. My chore was to remove the ticks from her. I would wait until they were grey and bulging, then pull them off and then burst them open with a stick. Big, bloody, juicy ticks. Their blood is purple, and it stains.

Perched on my rock, I talked to God about my dad. I asked Him to send me a sign, to let me know if my dad was okay. I worried that if indeed our father wanted to find us, he'd have no idea where to look, so I'd ask God to pass along the information. The seasons came and went, and never a word from our father.

I started referring to him as Bill, like the grownups around me did. It helped mark time, measured distance.

In school, I daydreamed that my father was a spy who was on a secret mission, or held captive by the Russians. Other times I'd imagine he was off somewhere feeding starving children in the desert, like the little kids from the television infomercials. Often I imagined he was dead; sometimes this made me feel better, because it made sense. If kids at school asked me, the new girl, about my dad, I'd tell them he was somewhere with Jesus, probably in Russia, but possibly dead.

By day in school, and each night after my bath, I aimed to please and control people and my surroundings. I made sure Mammaw saw me praying, because this made her happy. I refused to accept anything less than an A+ in my schoolwork, because this made my mother happy. I remember once receiving a simple "A" and running from the classroom into the hallway so no one would see me cry. In school, it was important for me to know the answers. All of them. The school counselor would sometimes pull me from class, rub circles on my back, and ask if everything was okay. I never told her I was thinking about death, resurrection, swimming, drowning, praying, making sure I went to heaven, wondering what we did to make my dad leave. I never told her how blurry the "A" without the plus sign looked through my angry tears. I only said what I thought she wanted to hear: that I was fine. I saved the truth for my rock. It was the only place where I could let go, be free.

On my rock, I breathed in the air, closed my eyes, and slipped away. I left my body and floated up high, then came back and walked home in time for dinner, often collecting a fresh bag of bones along the way.

In my mind, I was an archeologist. I loved searching for the bones, loved the their weight and texture in my hand. No one questioned my bone collecting. The only rule was I had to keep them outside on the front porch. The porch had a window that opened to the family room. While cataloging my treasures I played music, danced and sang along with Michael Jackson and Lionel Richie as I separated cow bones from deer, rabbit from dog. When people dropped their dogs off in the country to die, our home was often their final sleep.

I once left a bone on my rock. I decorated the bone with tick blood, so thick and purple. I did this as a test for God. If my bone disappeared, it would help prove that God and my dad really existed, that the echoes of the doorbell were heard, the answers coming.

I placed the bone on the edge of my rock, and there it stayed.

7
THE COMPOSER
Soundtrack: "Carrie Anne" – The Hollies

The following week, I arrive, CD's in hand. Once again, Bill is outside waiting for me.

"Hey Care!" Walking up to my car, he peers inside and shakes his head in disapproval. "This is such a nice car; you keep it a mess, though."

Ignoring his comment, "I brought your music." Three discs, 56 songs. He gives me a hug as soon as I step forward, accepts the CD's, and scans the song list, beaming.

"I can't wait to hear these songs, Care. Some of these I haven't heard in a long, long time." He flicks his half-smoked cigarette into the grass as we head inside. Dorothy's sitting in her chair, TV on, just like last week. She looks over and gives me a big smile, though it's clear by her eyes that she doesn't recognize me, and probably never will.

"Mom," Bill shouts, "I'm gonna turn this off for a bit, play some music." She smiles and nods toward the one man she recognizes and trusts, looks at me again and chirps, "He takes good care of me." I notice her teeth aren't slipping, but the baby head still hangs in the kitchen. I shiver.

I watch Bill fiddle with his outdated disc player, crank up the volume, step back and close his eyes. Once again I am a child. This is the same posture he would assume when I was a little girl. I would sit on the floor and watch him take on the role of conductor. Back then he'd play vinyl, placing the needle on the record ever so gently. Click, close his eyes. Snap, inhale. "Listen to this, Care." I'd watch his arms lift as the music began. I'm watching him now, 30 years later, the song and dance man, when not singing and dancing, conducting. I knew then, as I know now, not to speak, just to watch and listen. I stand, observing, tracing the notes as they pulse through his veins and bleed into the room.

Dorothy dances in her chair, eyes closed, bopping from side to side. Bill is lost in the music, and as the song fades he drops his arms theatrically, opens his eyes and exclaims, "Goddamn it that's go-oo-oood!" His joy fills the air. I breathe it in. Dorothy blushes.

"High school days Care. That song says high school days for me. Those were the days! And, of course, I also love it because of you." "Carrie Anne" by the Hollies. The song I'm named after. On Bill's list, there was a little asterisk next to this song title: *DIDN'T PUT FOR YOU, PUT IT BECAUSE I

DON'T HAVE IT. I wasn't sure how to take that; was he trying to be funny?

While many of the titles on Bill's list were sad songs, overall it was an interesting mix. Every song was beautiful and meaningful in its own way, a glimpse into his heart and mind. "Memories" - Elvis; "Things I Should Have Said" - the Grassroots; "Green Tambourine" - the Lemon Pipers; "Only Time" - Enya; kd lang's version of "Hallelujah." "You Got It" - Roy Orbison; "Why" - Annie Lennox; "Time After Time" - Cyndi Lauper; "Oh Very Young" - Cat Stevens; "Tide Rushes In," "In Your Wildest Dreams," and "I Know You're Out There Somewhere" - the Moody Blues; "Go Your Own Way" - Fleetwood Mac; "I'll Be Easy" - Earl Conley; "Sunday Morning Coming Down" - Ray Price (Bill's other side note: *NOT THE JOHNNY CASH VERSION, THE RAY PRICE VERSION); "I Started a Joke" by the Bee Gees, "Like a Rock" by Bob Seger; "Cherish" by the Association; "I'll Stand By You" - the Pretenders.

We listen to the first disc while Bill cooks for us: eggs, sausage, toast, and a big ole glass of milk. Same meal as last week, except he eats this time. After breakfast, we take another trip to the grocery.

When we return, Dorothy is sleeping in her chair. Careful not to wake her, we unpack the groceries in silence and then head outside for a smoke. Click. Snap. Plastic chairs. Same routine as last week. Without asking, he hands me one too. Click. Snap. Sigh.

"I'll listen to rest of those songs later in my room, with headphones on. I can't really crank my music here like I like to. Mom likes her TV. I miss my music. Well, I shouldn't say I miss it, because I still enjoy it. I just can't play it here like I used to, you know, because Mom, whenever she's not watching TV she's sleeping. And she watches TV and sleeps a lot, so I can't really rock and roll. Thanks again for those CD's, Care. I can't thank you enough."

I embrace the cheap cigarette like an old friend; watch the smoke waft through the air and merge with Bill's. "I enjoyed making the CD's; there are some great songs on there. I also made a bonus CD for you. Some music I like; current stuff I thought you might enjoy." I remove the fourth CD from my purse and take another drag. I feel nauseous, and the nicotine does not calm my nerves. In fact, it pulls them a little tighter. Bill thanks me for the CD and scans the titles and artists that are unfamiliar to him. Bon Iver, the National, Wilco, Edward Sharpe, Beck, Elliott Smith, Radiohead. His face looks open; his voice shimmers as he speaks. Music heals.

"Yep, you definitely get your love of music from me, Care. And your good looks. Both good traits." He winks. "I hope I don't see any other bad ones in future visits."

"Thanks, I guess." I stand up to crush my cigarette out on the ground, then immediately sit back down because I am so light-headed the dirt is sparkling. "So, what's new with you? Did you see the doctor yet about the alien baby?" I wish I had gum in my purse. The words stink as they leave my mouth.

"No honey, I used that money to fix my tooth.

A man's gotta eat." He snaps his teeth. "How's the turntable? Is she working for you? Play any good albums on her yet?"

"Oh yeah, she works. I love her. The first album I listened to was the Beatles, 'Love Songs'."

"That's a damn good choice. I miss her. I miss looking at her. I know she's in good hands. Take good care of her." He repeats, "I miss her."

"Grandma seemed to like the music. Did you see her grooving in her chair?"

"Yeah, she's still got it in her, tires easily, but yeah, she's good. It's been a good week."

"I remember her being around when I was little." Where my dad went, Dorothy went, or so it seemed when I was young. Now older, I can see that where Dorothy went, Bill often followed, with the exception of the years he was married. He always lived near or with his mom.

"Yeah. We're close. Course if I didn't look after her, who would?" I nod in agreement, but we both know she is taking care of him, too.

"I don't remember your dad at all. Did I ever meet him? What was he like?" His face closes, his lips and brows furrow as a stormy memory clouds his face.

"I remember little things Care, different things. Never having any money, having our water turned off at times, my dad out drinking, not paying the bills, our electricity turned off, having to move for reasons like that. I think that's why my oldest brothers, Mike and Danny, said 'I'm outta here' and left me there. Left me all their hand-me-down clothes, that was nice. But I wasn't, I wasn't close to my father. He would come to watch me play baseball a couple of times, I remember that. We moved every year. Different house, different school. Every single year."

"So your dad had a drinking problem?" My father loved his martinis, his permanent props when he was conducting. It was rare to see him without one, even while driving.

"Yeah, you could say that." He looks out into the distance. "His drinking problem was to the point where he wouldn't go to work. You know, I enjoy drinking. I enjoy my beer and stuff, but I didn't miss work or go off to the bar at eight o'clock in the morning—which is why we didn't have money to pay the bills and stuff, and had to move a lot, so... always moving...house to house, school to school. Yep, Michael and Danny went into the Air Force, I think Danny and I are the only two who graduated from high school. And the girls, the twins, they just did their own thing. My dad's lifestyle killed him. His liver was shot, but he eventually died from emphysema."

This was his fraternal grooming. The pattern he repeated unconsciously. Where he learned how to just get up and leave. He left, and in his absence my mom never had any money. So we moved from house to house, city to city; wore hand-me-down clothes from strangers and ate food from charity. It's easy, and understandable, for Bill to blame his father's drinking, explaining away the constant upheaval and instability. I, on the other hand, can't do the same for my dad.

"My mom actually remarried after my dad

died, you know. She married a man named Leo, moved to Tennessee with him, I lost track of her for a bit. My brothers and sisters and I were never close—maybe see them once every three or four years. Sometimes we go even longer than that. No one's heard from Danny in fifteen years, that's just the way my family is. My brother Mike, he lives right down there." I can see the trailer where his brother lives. Then he adds, "Course I'm pissed at him, you'd think a brother could be a little nicer, but oh well, he can just stay there, I don't care."

He does.

"He lives right down the street. Figure that out. It's a weird fucking family, Carrie. That's an easy way of putting it. Half the family lives nearby and nobody sees each other. There's no reason for that."

Half my life you lived close to me, but I never saw you. There's no reason for that.

"So... were you guys all alone? Who took care of you?"

"Yep. I remember if I missed the bus I'd have to hitchhike to school. And if no one picked me up, it was a very long walk." Click. Snap. I resist the urge to bum another cigarette, and thankfully he doesn't offer.

I can't believe little Dorothy, currently slip-sliding away in her chair, just left too. "Well, obviously you graduated, and with a scholarship, right?"

"Yeah. I did." He replies, smoke dangling from his lips. "You change one thing, you change everything. I always loved singing, acting, the applause and crap, you know. I can get choked up, all soft inside, when I hear or see someone sing a beautiful song, it gets me all warm. You have to have that in order to appreciate music; you have to feel it to perform it. I have that, least I think I do. I mean, I did. Hell, I don't know anymore." He shrugs and flicks his cigarette ash on the ground.

"Yep, I threw away a scholarship because I didn't want to take ballet with the boys…although I really enjoyed watching the gals do their routines, the guys started to get on my nerves. They talked funny and acted funny, and I just couldn't handle it. So I quit."

"Then what?"

"Well, I left the bright lights and mirrors of college for a full-time job, that's what. I made baking pans and cooking stuff for the military. I was bored, so I sped things up, until one day I kept my hand in the press too long and cut off the tip of my finger. I missed a couple days of work, went back and knew I was going to quit."

He pauses to relight his smoke. Click. Snap. I look for the missing tip of his finger.

"Here's the killer though, Care. When I gave notice, the company offered to send me to college for an electrical engineering degree and let me work part-time nights in quality control. So, here we go again—free college, a solid job, and your dad, the idiot, said no."

"Jesus," is all I can say, unable to hide my disbelief.

"Yep, as I said before, you change one thing you change everything. So then, I took a job downtown at Western Southern, and you know what happened next? I met the blonde."

"Mom?"

"Yep." Again he laughs, which makes him start coughing, but his face opens back up, the storm cloud dissipates. There is no doubt he loved my mother. "Did she ever tell you I was late for our wedding?"

"No."

"Yeah, I overslept, had to literally run into the building. I also had holes in my shoes. I was so late, I put on the wrong pair. Just a runnin'... I loved your mom. I couldn't believe she was marrying me."

Silence as he remembers their wedding day. I sit with the 'you change one thing you change everything' thought some more. Dorothy interrupts my inner visions—floating hallways, silent doors, confusing choices, sliced fingertips, and dizzying ballet—when she pokes her head out the front door. She takes one step onto the porch, looks around, and chirps, "Oooh, I should probably head back in." My dad stares at his mom like he is watching a movie he's seen dozens of times. Shaking his head, he explains. "She's scared of the outside. She used to go for walks, but now she just looks out the door from time to time." I see their similarities.

"You know that stuff I was telling you about my family before? I don't think anyone hates each other, but there's not a whole lot of love, either. There's just not a whole lot of love, Care."

"You love your mom. She loves you." As if on cue, Dorothy pokes her head out again. Hopping up from his chair, Bill heads towards his mother. "She must need me for something, she keeps looking for me."

I know how she feels.

As I wave goodbye to Dorothy, she waves back and squeaks, "Sure was nice to meet you. Come back soon before I die again."

"Die again?"

She waves me off, chuckling, "Oh, you know what I mean."

Bill walks me to my car, and I ask him, "Do you think having Alzheimer's is like dying each day? Like, every day, you wake up brand spanking new again? Could that be what it feels like for her?"

"Hell, I don't know Care, that's too many questions, that's too deep for me. Maybe. I do know she knows who I am, and that you only got one mom."

And one dad. At thirty-five, I'm just meeting mine. Driving home, I listen to Bill's playlist and think about what it took to get me here: homophobia, the tip of his finger, and no one showing him how to love, only how to leave.

On my way back home, I stop at a record store and pick up a new album. I shower before the boys arrive, to center myself and cleanse the day away. Later, as I read *The Odyssey* aloud, they both groan and then eventually fall asleep. The night is still bright, and I keep reading aloud to the unresponsive room, hoping the classic tale will tranquilize me as well, but it doesn't. I consider calling Mom or Twig to tell them I've been talking to Bill, but I don't. When Fixer texts to ask about my day, I debate telling him all that I've learned so far. But I don't. Instead, I melt into an extra long yoga practice. Afterwards I head downstairs to the still unfamiliar living room, place the National's *High Violet* LP on the turntable, and email Kentucky—sharing the progress of my journey, pausing from time to time to flip the spinning record.

8
LATCH KEY
Soundtrack: "Missing You"- John Waite

In 1984, we left the farm. Our time was up. My mother and grandmother had carried each other through their respective grief, and then it was too much. They each needed their privacy, their own beds. So my mother moved us into an apartment in town, right next door to our new school. No more exploring the woods. Now I zipped right home, key on a string around my neck. No stopping to play; no dog, no woods, no bones. Just get inside, lock the door, and wait for Mom to get home.

"Girls, if anyone knocks on the door do not answer it. Don't answer the phone, and if you happen to, and someone asks if your parents are home, what do you say?"

"Yes, they're here but they can't come to the phone right now, can I take a message?" Twig and I knew our lines.

"Good. Make sure you say they, not she. Just, really remember not to answer the door or the phone. Door most importantly." Our mother reviewed the rules with us constantly, paranoid about leaving us alone after school each day. Adam Walsh—ten years old, the same age as me—had disappeared in New York City, his horrific story made into a TV movie. My mother cried just thinking about him, telling us how she would just die if anything ever happened to either of us. We had to swear to never ever talk to strangers.

Twig was content to watch TV every afternoon, but I was going stir-crazy. I felt trapped. I longed to be outside; wanted to be alone instead of feeling lonely. I didn't want to watch shows about "together families," like The Cosby Show and Family Ties. Yet I didn't want to watch shows about families that were apart, One Day at A Time or Facts of Life. I liked to watch the news, until the day I heard the newscaster talk about 'latch-key kids', a label I immediately despised.

I watched the news coverage of famine in Ethiopia. While my mother cried thinking about Adam, I cried thinking about all the starving children. I was hungry too, but they reminded me I had enough to survive. I was lost too, but not like Adam.

Confined indoors, Twig found comfort in her TV shows. I missed the bones and fresh air; I missed singing and music. So we came to a family agreement: Twig had TV after school, I played music on the eight-track and turntable after dinner.

Using a bronze candle snuffer as a microphone, I often performed for my mother and sister. My mother loved it when I sang "Gloria" by Laura Branigan. Twig was fond of "Girls Just Wanna Have Fun." My go-to karaoke song? "Missing You" by John Waite. Go figure. I began to acquire my own LP's and 45's—Madonna, Prince, Van Halen, the Police, the Footloose soundtrack, Tears For Fears, Eurythmics, the Cars—and played them non-stop. This satisfied a part of me.

This new existence was such a contrast to the bright freedom of the farm. Everything around me was gray: the gray school, the gravel parking lot in front of our apartment, where our gray Chevette sat parked. The key around my neck and the free meal card I had to carry to school and get punched every morning and afternoon: both gray. I hated that card more than I hated the key. Even the cat that lived in the crawlspace under our building was gray. I knew I wasn't allowed to be outside, but once I caught sight of her, I couldn't help but break the rules. I named her Kitty, fed her, and coaxed her out from hiding. She was feral, but she grew to like and trust me. Like me, she was hungry, lonely, living in a crawlspace. She gave birth often, and let me hold her babies. I loved watching her nurse them, the tiny, crying kittens kneading her belly, fighting for both milk and space. Watching them grow was fascinating. Inevitably, I'd walk outside one day and they'd all be gone. Soon, she'd deliver a fresh batch and the cycle would start over.

I sat on the back porch behind our apartment every day. It became my new rock. Stroking Kitty replaced the bone collecting. With eyes open, I'd survey my new surroundings and then close them tight, straining to feel some comfort like my rock used to bring.

I knew we were poor when we lived on the farm, but I didn't truly feel its effects until we moved away. Most of the kids in line didn't have a gray card to punch. I got two free meals a day, breakfast and lunch. I began to enjoy the metallic flavor of the orange juice in the tiny little containers, the plastic aftertaste of the sausage, the nothingness of the spongy eggs. I ate only what I needed to survive, feeling thankful yet guilty for each meal. Though the free meal card embarrassed me, with every bite I saw children in Africa dying, heard kittens crying, so I learned to accept it.

My dream of my dad and Jesus and their martinis became a faded memory. Swimming felt too free, too blue. I no longer knew what to believe. Despite my prayers and my rock offering, there was no word from Bill. It had been four years. I quit praying. I began questioning. I got in trouble in Sunday school and CCD class. I went to confession frequently, where I lied to the priest and hummed my way through penance.

We still went to the farm to visit Mammaw. She'd cook one of her two specialties—fried spam sandwiches or chicken à la king (white toast, cut-up chicken breast on top, smothered in cream of mushroom soup and served with a side of green beans… voila!). But it wasn't the same. I felt like only a visitor. The bones had been cleared away from the porch. The fence between my former home and my hill seemed taller. The farm's magic was gone.

The only time I felt light was when my mom would take us to her friend's house. Kentucky's mom was her best friend, and she often babysat us when my mom had evening plans. Their home reminded me of the farm because it sat on top of a hill—remote and isolated. I liked the view, loved feeling my body ascend as we drove up their driveway. There, I could go outside and see nothing but land. And there was so much food Twig and I couldn't believe it. Little Debbie's, Capri Suns, Chips Ahoy cookies, sugary cereal… the type of food I would have wanted in my lunchbox at school, if I'd had a lunchbox. Kentucky and I would retreat to his room and listen to *Purple Rain* on his record player. While the music played his mom and dad cooked dinner for everyone—not chicken à la king or spam, thankfully.

***

I knew not to talk to strangers, but is a neighbor a stranger? I saw him daily after I broke the rule and began sitting outside. He sat on his back porch, alone, smoking cigarettes. He lived in the building next door, which looked exactly like ours. The apartment building was designed to look like one glorious mansion, with white pillars and shutters and a single door. You open the single door and that's where the façade crumbled. Two apartments below, two above. The staircase belonged to no one.

Sometimes I'd catch him watching us from his

front window as we walked home from school. Remembering Adam, I would shudder but then stare right back. I memorized every detail of his face so that if he snatched a child, I could describe him. When I began to wonder if that child could be me, or worse, Twig, I stopped going outside after school. Instead, I snuck Kitty inside and we hunted for information. Even without the bones, I was still an archeologist. I searched my mother's bedroom, initially for clues to my dad's whereabouts; a phone number, a scrawled letter, something, anything. All I found were her birth control pills, Jackie Collins novels, and a Catholic guide to reproduction.

Using simple juvenile sketches for the human body, the Catholic guide talked about waiting for marriage, putting God first, how to talk to your children about where babies came from (love, of course…) and other virtuous instructions. I preferred the Jackie Collins novels. They were far more interesting. My first read was *Lovers and Gamblers*. My second, *Chances*. I was obsessed. At ten years old, I'd already figured out what they told you to do, and what people actually did, were two very different things.

***

Valentine's Day, the darkest part of winter. My mother wasn't feeling well and asked me to take out the trash.

Terrified of the dark, I tiptoed to the dumpster across the parking lot, careful not to make a sound or produce a shadow. When I stopped to lift the dumpster's lid, the gravel was still crunching.

As the dumpster's lid slammed down, he greeted me. Hello. His voice was weaker than I had imagined. He stood right beside me, a bag of trash in one hand while his other hand hissed in his pocket. I thought of Adam. Surely he was going to chop me into little bits and throw me into the dumpster. From his jacket pocket he pulled out a small, heart-shaped box of chocolates, the generic kind from the drugstore. "I got you these for Valentine's Day." I accepted his gift—his hand grazing mine for a brief moment—mumbled "Thank you," then turned and walked away slow. If I ran he would know I was terrified. His gaze followed me until I closed the fake front door of our dwelling. Up the stairs I ran.

I waited until I got to my bedroom, where I pulled the box of chocolates out from beneath my shirt, crying as I devoured every last tasteless piece. Snot, saliva and tears dripped from my face as I ate and wept. I hid the empty heart-shaped box between my mattresses and cried myself to sleep, terrified and sick to my stomach. My rock seemed so very far away.

9
RESURRECTION
Soundtrack: "Your Wildest Dreams" – The Moody Blues

Christmas 1986. I am almost eleven. Twig and I asked Santa for Cabbage Patch Dolls. I felt guilty asking for something I knew Mom couldn't afford. It was another test, this time to see if Santa was real or not. I suspected he wasn't. I could see it in my mother's bones, working two jobs during the holidays. I can only imagine how exhausting it must have been to be the mom, the dad, the Easter Bunny, the Tooth Fairy… the hardest of all, Santa.

Twig and I freaked out, couldn't believe we got our wish. My Cabbage Patch Kid came with the name Gertie Bliss. Gertie, a name meaning strong spear; Bliss, meaning joy, happiness. And we each got a stroller, outfits for our babies, and diapers that smelled like sunshine.

I also got a hamster. I named her Holly. Mom knew I missed the farm and Whiskey the dog. She knew I was lonely. She suspected I was bringing Kitty inside, even though Mom was allergic. This was a way to solve both problems.

We were still in disbelief that we'd gotten our wish when the phone rang late Christmas evening. I was already in bed with Gertie tucked beneath my arm, losing myself in the heavenly scent of her woven flesh, when the sound of the phone ringing tickled my sixth sense. Twig woke up, too. We knew instinctively it was him.

We ran into the living room, just as we had that morning in our eagerness to see what was beneath the synthetic tree. Our mother beat us to the phone, as if she'd been waiting for it to ring. Nevertheless, she looked stunned, bewildered as she picked up the receiver. After trying in vain to shoo us back to our rooms, she gave up and allowed each of us to say hello. Twig went first, as I clutched Gertie tight. My mother sat on the couch with her hands covering her mouth, her eyes following invisible trails across the floor.

I recognized his voice at once, my entire body hurting at the sound of it. His laugh was still the same… the same laugh that disappeared underwater, taunted me in my poolside dream. I remember thinking it was strange for him to be laughing while I was feeling like my heart was on fire. I was confused, thrilled and terrified, feeling and sounding like I was underwater as I said "Hello."

"It's your old Dad, sweetie. I wanted to wish

you a Merry Christmas. So, Merry Christmas! What'd Santa bring you?"

Had he sent the money for the dolls?

It had been almost six years. Six years of waiting, hoping, praying. Maybe I had been asking the wrong person all along. First the Cabbage Patch Dolls, now this.

Santa – 2, Jesus - zip.

"Your father is going to be in Cincinnati soon. He wants to drive down here and see you girls." The morning after the call, my mother's eyes were swollen with lack of sleep.

She sat at the foot of Twig's bed and told us our father was married. To Debi with an 'i'. Then she told us we had a little sister. Her name was Katie; she was two. He wasn't feeding babies in the desert, or acting as a spy, or being held captive by the Russians. He wasn't dead. He was married, with a new family. That possibility had never crossed my mind.

Arrangements were made; he would come to visit us in two weeks. At this announcement, I closed my eyes, clutched Gertie tight, and was transported straight back to my rock. A familiar numbness took over my body, and I fell fast asleep.

We waited by the window while our mother curled her hair. She'd dressed us in matching dresses—mine blue, Twig's pink. I strained to look across the gravel parking lot, secretly hoping the creepy man next door was still watching, so he could see I actually did have a dad.

His shiny red Cadillac pierced the gray landscape. The sun was setting as he stepped out of his car and surveyed our surroundings. I stood at the window, clutching Gertie tightly to my chest. Twig and I had both carefully dressed our Cabbage Patch Kids in their best outfits.

He stayed the night at our apartment. Before we were sent to bed, we sat beside him, watching the happy families on TV. Later, from our bedroom, Twig and I pressed our ears against the door. She fell asleep, but I listened as my parents made love on the couch.

The next morning, we drove to the mall so Bill could take us shopping. Again, we had just one day with him. Again, it was a Sunday. Again, my mother stayed behind. He smoked his cigarettes and played his favorite songs for us. His red Cadillac, shiny and clean and new, felt like a limousine compared to our tiny Chevette. It smelled like Juicy Fruit gum, Scope, cologne, menthol cigarettes, and leather.

"Ever hear of the Moody Blues?"

As I was in the front seat, it was my job to change the music, just like when I was little and was tasked with sliding the vinyl back into its case. I opened and closed cassettes at his request. Twig was in the back, her doll dancing along with the music. Gertie sat on my lap.

"The Moody Blues…" I scanned his collection for the title. "They sound familiar." I found the tape. He popped it in, then demanded, "Listen to this, girls, this is good stuff." I felt like I was floating in a magical musical time machine, where minutes stood still and memories were erased. Where people communicated through song.

Between musical assignments, I studied Dad's every move. He bobbed his head along with the music, I moved mine. His hands marked the beat on the steering wheel, I tapped my fingers on the cream leather seat. He smiled and pointed out whenever a certain lyric held special meaning. I listened. I understood.

I recognized the Moody Blues from the radio—Casey Kasem's Weekly Top 40 held more influence over me than any pulpit priest. When he sang along, I did too. He stopped conducting, turned the volume down, and glanced sideways, asking with a laugh, "Do you know what monotone means?" I didn't, but I stopped singing immediately and made a mental note to look it up when we got home. He turned the music back up, laughed again softly, and resumed conducting. I sat quiet and motionless.

He bought us new clothes at the mall, paid my mother for all the years of child support neglect. It was decided that he would come back in June, when school let out. We would spend part of the summer in West Virginia with him, Debi, and Katie. My mother gripped the kitchen counter as Bill delivered this news.

"You'll spend a few weeks this summer with your Dad and Debi," she repeated, her face stretched into a fake smile.

I wanted to be a part of that family, wanted to be Bill's daughter again, and meet my new little sister. I was already jealous of the time she had with him, time that had been taken from me. I was torn between my mother's pain and my longing for my dad.

He called often between January and June. We tried to talk to Katie, but she was too little to understand. Debi was always on the line. She sounded the same, still called me "Darlin."

After Christmas break, I remembered to look up "monotone" in the school dictionary.

Monotone: n. a single unvaried musical tone; a person unable to produce or distinguish between musical intervals.

To clarify, I asked my teacher what the word meant. She replied, "It means you can't sing."

Several years later, I read an article about the appeal of Cabbage Patch Dolls. The writer, a psychologist, had a theory that the Cabbage Patch craze was due to the fact that most children liked to fantasize they were adopted. Many children feel unloved or unwanted, out of place with society or their family. This feeling, the author stated, was perhaps created by the increase of the single parent family during the eighties. A child who adopted and loved a Cabbage Patch Kid could live out that fantasy, take care of the child, give it the family it deserved.

Sing to it, if need be.

10
JULIAN
Soundtrack: "Much Too Late For Goodbyes" –
Julian Lennon

Bill kept his other promise, and we spent the better
part of the summer of '87 in West Virginia, with
Dad and Debi and Katie. We stayed at Bill's
mother's house the night before we left, where we
finally met our little sister. Dorothy greeted us at the
door, waving her hands and exclaiming "Oh my
Gooodddd, it's been soooooo looonnng, oh loves
how I've missed you…" On and on she went,
smothering our faces against her big squishy bosom,
then back to take another look, then back to the
bosom again. She smelled funny, like Avon Skin-
So-Soft mixed with sauerkraut. Our sister Katie
bore a striking resemblance to my Cabbage Patch
Kid with her flaxen pigtails and dimpled cheeks.
Debi embraced us as if we were her long-lost

children, charmed us with 'Darlins' and smothered us with kisses. No one mentioned the obvious. No one apologized. It was as if those six long years had never happened.

It was during the West Virginia summer that I met Julian. I never learned his real name, but he looked like John Lennon's son, so I decided on Julian. He worked at the convenience store next to one of the Laundromats Bill and Debi co-owned with Debi's parents in West Virginia. Bill explained to Julian that I was his daughter, that I would be spending the summer with him, and that I would be over from time to time buying their cigarettes: Marlboro Reds and Newports for Dad, Salem Ultra Light 100's for Debi. Julian never questioned the morality of my purchases, despite the fact that I was only twelve. Sometimes I used the extra money to buy myself a pack of Salem's.

Their house in West Virginia was an old three-story Victorian, massive and full of secrets. Bill, Debi, and Katie lived on the third floor. They shared the home with Debi's parents, who inhabited the rest of the house. It was quickly determined that I was old enough to babysit Katie. When we weren't perming each other's hair or shopping for new clothes, I spent most of the summer with Katie—watching Welcome to Pooh Corner, snooping around the house and smoking my pilfered cigarettes whenever she napped.

Beautiful Julian. All long, wavy hair and muscles that rippled beneath the sleeves of his uniform. He talked very little, but smiled at me and once told me I had my father's eyes. When he said they were pretty, it sent an electric jolt down my spine.

It started innocently enough, my nighttime bathroom ritual. After dinner I would sneak cigarettes and matches up to the third floor bath, crack open the window, draw up the bathwater, and watch myself smoke in the mirror while waiting for the tub to fill. I loved to smell the unlit end of the cigarette before lighting it, inhaling the tobacco's sweet, mossy scent. I loved to stand in front of the mirror naked with the smoke dangling from my mouth, like Jesse James or Clint Eastwood. Sometimes I placed one hand on my hip, exhaling with a face devoid of expression, like Twiggy, the supermodel who'd inspired my sister's nickname. Other times I'd wrap my right arm around my waist, the crook of my left elbow resting on my right hand, just below my breasts, which were just beginning to make themselves known. I'd stare into the mirror, holding my cigarette just in front of my lips and squinting, like I was on the verge of saying something profoundly intelligent. Then, I'd hop in the bath, smoke another one, hop out, and go to bed.

Until the day I discovered the magazines. These were different from the Playboys he kept on the coffee table and in the guest room bookshelf. They were carefully hidden, but no match for my meticulous naptime snooping. Hustler, Penthouse, and a dozen other titles…he had them all. Along with my nighttime habit of smoking and bathing came a self-education on the real human anatomy. Lucky Santangelo came to life. I realized with a start that the sketches in the Catholic guide to sexuality were off—way off. A voracious reader, I actually read the articles and interviews, enjoyed the captions beneath the lewd cartoons. More often than not, just like everyone else, I looked at the pictures.

I suddenly became aware of how different my body looked in comparison to the models. Noticing the hairiness of my legs and arms, I used my father's razor to shave both. I unearthed Debi's suitcase of makeup, entranced by the false eyelashes and vivid colors. I glued on the lashes and caked my face in powder as my bathwater ran, then stared at myself in the mirror. The lashes were uneven, and poorly adhered. They made me feel both stupid and pretty.

Through it all, I thought of Julian.

I wanted to shed my tomboy skin, to grow up quick and pretty. I wanted Julian to notice me, to fall in love with me, to be my first kiss. I'd soak in the tub until the water turned cold, smoking, staring at the pictures, with a full face of makeup, eyelashes glued haphazardly, legs and arms peppered with razornicks. My dark hair floated and clung to the rim of the tub. The room was thick with smoke, my emotions and hormones swirling along with the bathwater.

I was both horrified and fascinated by the pictures. They were at once fascinating and terrifying. I wondered if Julian did those things. I wondered if all grown-ups did. I saw my father differently. Those were his magazines. I thought he was gross. I thought I was gross. Yet, I couldn't stop looking. I was still an archeologist, but instead of collecting bones I was searching for—addicted to?—porn and cigarettes.

My arms and legs, silky smooth each night, were rough and itchy by morning. I quickly learned that being a woman, maintaining certain imitation beauty, was hard work. Sex looks like a lot of different things, and hair itches when it grows back.

I couldn't have cared less about Gertie. It was my father who carried her to the car when we left to go home to our mother. Curious, slightly obsessed, and forever changed, I embraced a new passion: snooping. Everywhere I went, I continued to dig. Lots of people had things to hide, like sex and cigarettes.

That would be our first, and only, summer with my father's new family. The following year, Bill and Debi split up. We spent a week with Bill each of the next two summers. No longer supported by Debi and her family's businesses, he disappeared again. In 1990, when I was sixteen, he contacted us with an invitation to his third wedding. That visit was our last. He caught me smoking his cigarettes that time, and instead of yelling brought me home a pack. He also busted me trying to steal some of his magazines. A boy at school had offered me twenty-five dollars if I could get him the Playboy with Cindy Crawford. My dad told me that wasn't a fair price.

Debi remarried shortly after leaving Bill; Katie was adopted by her stepfather, and it would be a decade before we'd see her again.

My mother had remarried too, in 1986. Leaving behind the creepy neighbor and crawlspace apartment, we moved briefly to Lexington, and then back to my native Cincinnati in 1988, following our new stepfather's job opportunities. I didn't mind the first move, because it nudged us from poverty level up to the elusive middle class. No more free-lunch card; suddenly our pantry had the Little Debbies and other treats we could never afford before. I could also ride my bike around the neighborhood, and my longtime prayers for MTV were answered. But I would have given all that up to stay in Lexington. I'd made friends I loved, and didn't want to leave them. For this reason I grew to hate my mother's husband, and did whatever I could to make his life miserable. Sometimes I felt bad about the cruel things I said to my blink-and-you've-missed-him stepfather, but then I'd remember how he banned me from listening to Prince and forbade me from attending Madonna's *Who's That Girl* tour with my friends, and my hatred would bubble back to the surface. They split in 1988, shortly after the move to Cincinnati. I'm sure I had a lot to do with that.

My dad also ended up back in Cincinnati, after his third marriage tanked. But despite our close proximity, we never heard from him again.

11
PEGGY
Soundtrack: "Can't Take My Eyes Off Of You" –
the Four Seasons

During the almost two decades spent apart from my
father, I kept him close through music. It was like a
secret conduit, a cord I couldn't cut. Some of my
earliest and fondest memories are of him selecting a
record, smiling, placing it on the turntable, and
sharing his love of the song with me. I began
collecting my own vinyl when other girls my age
were collecting Barbies. Picking up used albums
from thrift shops, garage sales, and discount bins, I
wondered about the previous owners. What
secondhand memories was I inheriting? Why were
they discarded? I'd smell the vinyl, stroke the liners,
study the album covers and follow the lyrics as the
music played. Later, I'd encourage my own children
to close their eyes and listen, to absorb—just as I'd

been taught. Pay attention to the emotion, the rhythm and the lyrics, I'd say—echoing Bill's instructions. I tried to keep his good qualities and our happy moments alive, and ignored the rest.

Over the years, I often thought about contacting him to ask if he still collected vinyl. If anything, it seemed like a reasonable excuse for calling, a conversation starter. I feared if he said no, perhaps he had truly given up, let it all go, which worried me. I still wanted him to find happiness, and he couldn't have that without music. Worse still, I feared if he died, someone else would inherit all of those albums, my only happy memories of him. What I truly wanted was for him to call me, to ask me if I remembered. I wanted him to bequeath to me the one thing that wove us together innately. The Dreamer in me imagined a box arriving on my doorstep, with a letter informing me that my dad had passed away and left me all of his records. There would be a second letter, penned in his hand, an apology. Everything he never said. This imagined scene was both tragic and lovely. Of course, he never did call. Probably too proud, maybe too ashamed. Or perhaps he simply didn't care to call, didn't think about it.

Our next Sunday together, after breakfast and a trip to the grocery store, we head outside and I ask about his record collection. I'd spotted a few albums displayed in his home, a couple dozen at best, nowhere near the hundreds he once owned. He launches into his earliest memories as a child, of playing 78 rpm records on the old Victrola.

"Yeah, let's talk about the music, since it seems to be the tie that binds, huh Care?" I nod and smile, happy to have confirmation that he'd also felt that connection.

"I must have been six or seven years old. We lived on Eastern Avenue across from my elementary school. I don't recall anyone else in the family playing records as often as me. I have no idea what albums I bought when I started collecting; probably Johnny Mathis or early rock and roll. I do remember my first live concert. The Four Seasons, live at Cincinnati Gardens."

"I actually remember the very first record I purchased with my own money," I ventured. "*Purple Rain*. I still have it."

Smiling in approval, he continues, "Yep. There's certain firsts you never forget—your first record, first job…everyone remembers their first job. And their first love, of course. That goes without sayin'. All of mine happened at the same time."

"Oh, yeah?"

"I worked at a movie theater, at the concession stand. But then I got promoted; the highlight of that 'career' was when I got to run the projectors. It was a fluke really. The guy who was hired to do it either never showed up or called in sick fairly often, so they had to teach me how to run the projector as backup. I looked forward to him not showing up so I could be big time and control the movies. The job afforded me my bike, gave me drug store money, and most importantly… I could start buying vinyl records. Yep. I was 'Big Time!'"

Big Time Bill the showman. The job seemed fitting, for I can see my father's life, like a series of scenes from a movie reel, when he tells me stories. I can see him riding his bike, buying candy and records, coasting to his job, wind in his hair, all set to the soundtrack of music in his head. Every good movie has a score and a leading man.

"What about your love?" I ask as we settle into the plastic chairs in front of his trailer. "Your first love was the records?"

"No, honey, that was Peggy. She had dark brown hair and freckles and a smile everyone loved. A smile you'd see drawn on a cartoon character; just a really big happy smile. She was dating a boy who worked there too—he had a car. But I won her over even without a car, you see," he says, leaning back into his plastic chair and giving me a wink, still proud of himself. He pauses to light a smoke. Click, Snap.

I wink back, and pull out one of my own cigarettes. Vowing to only smoke on Sundays, I had caved and bought a pack. They are imports from Europe, their 'quality' somehow justifying my desire. He hands me his Zippo casually without looking, and as it clicks open I pause and watch the flame flicker. Snap.

Inhale, exhale. I lean back into my plastic chair. "So what won her over, your charm?"

"Nope. We're talkin' about music, remember? That was the way to her heart. I would buy albums and pass them on to her, and she would write on the liners, underline favorite lyrics, circle and comment on favorite titles, and then give them back to me.

That's how we communicated, how the romance began. The music won her over."

So beautiful. I am in love with this story. I see Peggy. I am Peggy. "So, where's all your music now?"

"They're gone, Care. Long gone. My records, along with everything else I owned, were sold to some man after I failed to pay rent on a storage unit. Everything. Clothes, records, movies, photographs, everything… all my memories. All gone." He motions to the wind, takes a long drag off his cigarette. We sit in silence, watching our smoke rings intermingle.

Gone. The last thing I wanted to hear. I want him to have those albums with Peggy's notes and hearts and circles. I want him to listen and remember all those pretty things. I want to listen with him. I want that piece of him when he's gone, when the alien baby finally takes him away. I no longer feel selfish asking him for those records, and now it is too late. I take another drag of my cigarette, and before I can stop myself, the words escape my mouth in a cloud of smoke.

"Dad, how come you never called me?"

"Oh Care, let's not go there today. Might upset the baby. I'm done talking."

I feel like he's just slammed a door in my face. Stunned by his sudden curtness, I stand and start to pack my things. He doesn't stop me. The alien baby is hovering, cutting our visit short, feeding my anger through the cord that will always connect us. I need to leave. Fast. He flicks his cigarette into the dirt and gives me a quick hug goodbye, taking control of the situation by saying he needs to call it a day, go inside to rest. "Alien baby."

I drive home in defeated silence, and take what's become my ritual post-visit shower followed by an extra long yoga session, which has taken on a whole new level of necessity. The boys won't be home for hours. Shakespeare leaves me a voicemail, wondering if I have time for dinner, but I ignore his message. Kentucky sends me an email, subject: in the burden of the sun, a response to a Suzanne Vega song I'd sent him the day before. I don't even open it. Fixer sends me a text, wanting to talk when he brings the boys home. I respond that I'm not feeling well. Alien baby.

12
SHAGGY
Soundtrack: "Old Man" – Neil Young

His name was Shaggy. (Not really, but he was long and lanky and a complete stoner with an insatiable appetite, so Shaggy seemed to fit.) Like Peggy, he too had brown hair and freckles and a cartoon smile that took over his entire face.

We met late in the summer of 1989. Fourteen going on twenty, I had finally settled into Cincinnati, having gotten past my initial hatred. Shaggy lived across the street from one of my friends, another latchkey kid. My new friends and I spent a lot of time together; the kids whose parents aren't home after school always seem to find each other. One of my friends had a pool, so we typically gathered at her place. We would sip wine coolers in our bikinis, sunbathing while listening to the radio. It was the summer of Debbie Gibson and Milli

Vanilli—"Girl You Know It's True," "Lost In Your Eyes"; Paula Abdul and Bobby Brown—"My Prerogative," "Straight Up." I was fond of the one-hit wonders—Boy Meets Girl's "Waiting For A Star To Fall," Martika's "Toy Soldier," and Neneh Cherry's "Buffalo Stance."

From my friend's pool deck, we could watch Shaggy and his friends playing basketball. I told my friends I had a secret crush on him, and announced my intention to give him my virginity, which made them all gasp and stare wide-eyed, wondering if I was joking. I wasn't. I'd made the decision months ago, after watching him skip class and then return to school with a McDonald's bag in hand, an admirably bold act of rebellion. I had smiled at him from within the confines of my algebra class. He had replied with a wink and a wild grin.

One day, emboldened by too many drinks, one of my girlfriends whistled and screamed loud enough for him to hear, "Carrie loves you!" Not long after, the doorbell rang. When I answered, he extended his hand, blinded me with a dazzling smile, and said, "I hope you're Carrie." He was seventeen and drunk. I was fourteen and in deep.

Less than two months later, on a blanket in his backyard, I kept the promise I'd made. Lying up at the stars, I wondered if I looked any different, if anything essential to my being had changed, because I still felt the same.

Thursday night, just before Labor Day weekend, 1990, Shaggy knocked on my bedroom window, like he often did. He had gone to a concert.

James Taylor. I had given him the tickets, and waited for his familiar tap afterwards. My two best friends from Lexington were in town for the holiday weekend. The plan was for all of us to sneak out together that night—go pool hopping, drink beer, smoke weed. Shaggy had a friend with him, and it appeared they'd both been drinking. They tried to persuade us to leave, but as we watched both boys stumble and take a piss in my front yard, we refused.

I asked Shaggy how much they'd had to drink. He called me a bitch, asked was I his mother, told me to fuck off. We had fought in the past, but he had never called me names, never spouted obscenities. I refused to leave and he refused to come in, even though my girlfriends and I asked them to come inside instead—hang out, watch a movie. We woke my mother with our arguing and as she called my name from her bedroom Shaggy was walking away, giving me the finger. I returned the gesture, slammed my window shut and took the phone off the hook, but not before screaming across the yard that I never wanted to speak to him again. I apologized to my mother for waking her, then spent the rest of the evening horrified and embarrassed.

The next morning, the moment I placed the phone back on the receiver, it rang. I figured it was him, calling to apologize, but when I picked up, his mother was on the line.

She asked if I had gone to the concert with her son. I said yes, which was a lie, but he often used me as a cover when he was actually going out with friends. She asked me if I was with him after the concert. I answered yes, which wasn't a lie. "Did he bring you home after the concert?" "Yes." More lying. She asked me what time. "10:30ish..." Partial lie; that was the time he'd appeared at my window. She asked me who was driving the car. My silence confirmed what she already knew—that I had been lying about the evening. Then she told me he was dead. Both boys were dead. The car had crashed into a telephone pole at the bottom of a hill on Eight Mile Road.

Eight Mile Road. If you turn left out of my subdivision, that's the street you're on.

I passed out and fell to the floor, waking my mother. When I came to, she was kneeling beside me, talking to Shaggy's mom on the phone. *What concert? No, she was here all evening...* By noon, my house had turned into an impromptu visitation. Everyone I knew from school was there. Everywhere I turned were eyes staring, ears straining, arms extending, hearts breaking. Most were my friends, Shaggy's friends; all were curious and horrified. I felt their pity and shared their shock.

Though tears were flowing, none of them were mine. In shock, I couldn't feel a thing except vomit hovering below my throat. The previous evening was on constant replay in my mind, a tormenting reel. I kept hearing the last words I had said to him: that I never wanted to speak to him again.

I slipped away to my bedroom. I travelled to my hill, my body numb. When I awoke, it was dark, the house was quiet, and my mother was sitting on the edge of my bed, waiting for me to awaken.

"It's okay to cry," she said, unable to hold back her own tears. She handed me a small blue pill and a glass of water.

Days, hours, sometime later—time meant nothing, since I slept and cried my way through the cycles of the moon and the sun—my mother told me Shaggy's parents needed to speak to me. I was the last person to see their son alive. Along with this news, she delivered another blue pill. Dutifully, I swallowed it. They would come to bring such comfort, the sweet, forgiving Valium. My new blue Love. Erasing the tears by day and filling my nights with rich Technicolor dreams.

In their living room, I told his parents what I knew. I told them I gave their son the tickets to the James Taylor concert. I told them about the fight and his refusal to come inside. I told them I could tell he'd been drinking.

They told me the impact from the crash made it impossible to determine who was driving. The engine alone was thrown forty feet from the car. Neither of them was wearing their seatbelts.

I wanted to tell them I was sorry. Wanted to apologize for every lie we ever told them. That I was desperate to turn back time. But I didn't, and I couldn't—the Valium kept me still and silent.

Instead, I asked if I could go to his bedroom. I wanted to smell him, to touch his belongings. They let me. His presence lingered in his room, his woodsy scent—a combination of incense, sweat, and cigarettes laced with marijuana and a hint of Irish Spring soap. I walked to his window, the one I had climbed out of so many times, often escaping just as his parents were waking. I opened it, closed it. I went to his closet and ran my hands over his clothes—his soccer jerseys, his Grateful Dead tees. Sobbing quietly, so our mothers didn't hear. I caught a glimpse of myself in the mirror. I hadn't brushed my hair or teeth in days. My eyes were crimson, glazed and puffy—proof that, despite the Valium, I'd done some weeping when no-one was looking. I wondered idly, with no particular concern, how long I'd been wearing the same clothing.

On his dresser was a cassette, a mix tape I had made for him. His mother told me the tape had been pulled from the wreckage, said I could have it back if I wanted. I tucked it into my back pocket, along with a pack of Camel Lights he had hidden in his sock drawer. I left, shutting the door softly without looking back.

Back home, I went to my room and put the cassette tape into my stereo. I opened the window and lit one of his cigarettes, no longer bothering to hide the smoke from my mom. I pushed play and the tape resumed mid-song. "Old Man" by Neil Young.

I tortured myself by imagining Shaggy listening to this song, and then dying halfway through. I imagined him singing along, pausing to light a cigarette, crashing into a telephone pole. Alone, I cried hard. I couldn't stop if I'd wanted to. Shaking, chain smoking, rewinding, sobbing—not wanting to hear anything else but that song, over and over and over again.

I carried our mix tape wherever I went. I listened to it every day to and from school. I listened to it as I bummed rides from friends to the cemetery each week. I listened to it on the way to testify in court, for insurance reasons, that I was unaware of who was driving that evening. I listened to it every night as I fell asleep, and every morning as I got dressed, the torturous melodies still drifting in my head as I took another Valium and floated through the hallways of high school.

I shared this story, the story of my first love and his death, with my father the week after he told me about Peggy. He listened quietly, nodded, and then said, "You know, when I was driving from West Virginia to North Carolina via Cincinnati—I was swinging through Cincinnati to see my mom—I was driving early in the morning, listening to talk radio. It was a miracle I could receive the radio station, I was still pretty close to the West Virginia border. The newscaster said a couple of teenagers had died in an apparent drunk driving accident. I thought of you when he mentioned what part of town they were from, and where they went to high school. I thought about calling you."

He thought about calling me.

13
REGRET
Soundtrack: "Sunday Morning Coming Down" –
Ray Price

He thought about calling me. How I wish he had.
Would that one simple phone call, in a deep time of
need, have changed anything? At the very least I
would have known he cared, if only for a moment.
Shaggy's death triggered a depression that had been
lurking since I was a small child. I kept it hidden.
The Valium helped. I stayed on it for many years. I
did well in school, despite the fact that I did too
many drugs and went to too many parties and did
other things I'd quickly forget. I worked long hours
at my after-school job as a receptionist at a hair
salon, which I loved. It was stable and fun.

I perfected the art of going through the motions
when others were around, then sinking into madness
behind the scenes. Believing that people always
leave in one way or another, my pattern of

detachment was sealed. I could, and would, go on to fall in love again—but always at a distance, choosing partners who were not fully available, because I couldn't be. This arm's-length love gave me a false sense of safety and control. I do this still.

Even to this day, the only people who have breached my gated heart are my children. With them, I'm able to love without boundaries, and that is why I cling to them. It was at twenty-three, when my oldest son Logan was born, that I began to feel again. I may have given birth to him, but in many ways, he re-birthed me.

"I wish you would have called me. That would have been nice." It's Sunday, I'm back at Bill's, and this is the first time I allow him to see how much his absence broke my heart.

"I know, Care. I know. I made a lot of bad moves, there's so much I regret." There's no talking with his hands, no grand gestures, just a stare aimed straight ahead but looking backwards. There it is: the word he has avoided for years. The ugly feeling he's lived with for so long. The feeling that I believe has played a major part in the alien baby's conception, for how can you live with such heavy sadness, such loneliness and shame, and not suffer? The emotions, stifled for so long, have to manifest somewhere. After all, they don't just disappear.

Regret.

In releasing this word, is my father going into labor?

"I felt so bad about what happened with your mom and me. I was so angry, angry at myself. I wasn't a good husband. I was a terrible husband, actually. I won't get into details, because you don't need to know everything, but I was not a good husband, or father. I convinced myself I wasn't needed. I figured I didn't make much of an impression on you guys, and if I did it was a bad one, so I gave up. I split. It's my biggest regret."

The word gnaws and suckles, travels down the umbilical cord, feeds his alien baby.

"Not being there when you girls were growing up, that's my biggest regret of my entire life. I don't care what else my dumb decisions have brought me…" He gestures toward the trailer, the sky, makes a circle with shaky hands. His voice quiet, a whisper. "I look at you, and my only memories are from when you were a very small child. It's hard for me to accept the fact that you're thirty-five years old now. Where the hell did those years go? I missed them all."

His eyes are full of tears, and he looks down to avoid my stare, struggling to keep his composure. A gentle, cool breeze tries to caress us, but nothing can soothe the gaping wounds we share.

He stops to light a cigarette; a quieter Click, Snap cracks the stillness. "Those years, Care, those years, they're gone. You can't reclaim that time, and it hurts. You might find that hard to believe, but it hurts. Gone…"

Whispering, repeating 'gone', his cry is soft, internal. There is no drama to it, no dancing, no singing; it is quiet and heavy. Between his ragged breaths, I take his hand, unsure of how to comfort him.

He settles into the truth of what he has just said,

takes a deep breath, and for the first time looks straight into my eyes and asks, "What else you want to know, Care?"

"Anything you need to tell me."

"Your sisters, well, Twig, I'm not sure of her feelings for me. I'm sure she has ill feelings; I wouldn't hold that against her. I expect it, really. But it sure would be nice to see her more. It's nice she calls sometimes. I know she's busy and stuff, but if I could see my girls every week I couldn't be any happier. If I could turn back time, I'd die a happy man. Of course I know that's not possible. But to go so long and not see you, never know how you're doin', how your kids are, what they look like. I think about it more than you guys think I do. I really do… you, Twig, Katie."

It wasn't just me he left, nor was his disappearing act a one-time thing. He appeared and then vanished from all of our lives, over and over again, like a cruel magic trick.

I ask him about Katie, the little sister I met when I was twelve and she was two. I've seen her fewer than five times in my life. What would he say to her now?

"What would I say?" He repeats, looking upwards for an answer. "I have no idea. Certainly it's not a conversation I could have in a phone call. It's been twenty some odd years since I've seen her. I know she's my daughter, I wish I knew her. I'm sure there's so much confusion."

Confusion, indeed, though I cannot speak for my sisters. But it's as clear to me as the narrow lines of grass and dust that separate his trailer from the next—he saw one path, one direction, and it was always toward the exit. Like the sound of the Click Snap, it was definitive. Weeks ago, when his armor was still visible, he told me he was always fighting battles. Many times, his choices sparked his own personal wars. War is no place for children, so he left us behind.

I look at my father and try to see the young Bill, a vulnerable boy with large brown eyes. I see him living without his dad, on his own, making his way to school, stumbling without guidance, uncertain which way he should go, no one to ask, unaware that one day he would be saddled with regret.

"I'm glad that we're talking now, Care. I'm happy we've seen each other recently. That's a relief. If I go tomorrow, I know I've seen and talked to one of my girls, and hopefully answered her questions. Maybe you can let the others know how sorry I am. I'll never know if I truly have your forgiveness, or your love. Don't know if I can accept it, or forgive myself, but it's a relief just sitting here talking to you." He looks weak with relief, in fact—it's clear he'd been yearning to take off the armor. The labor pain subsides, if only for a bit. Pausing to wipe away tears, he then tells me, "You know you were planned, we were glad to have you. I changed your diaper, played with you, all the fun stuff dads are supposed to do. And I enjoyed every minute of it. You were all planned, I had good intentions."

"Thanks, Dad. That's nice to know." He wanted to be a dad, just didn't know how. This, somehow, I've always known.

"You know, there are so many songs that remind me of you girls. Care, you always used to sing. Sometimes I close my eyes and I can still hear your little voice singing. I miss my music. A lot of songs I like are sad songs, they tell stories. You like sad songs too. I noticed that listening to the CD you made me. That's some seriously sad music, Carrie. Songs bring back memories. I assume many of your memories are sad, too. I know I did some of that to you. I'm so sorry. You know, it all happened, so you go on. I've been up, I've been down… right now I'm down, but maybe I'll get back up again."

His words sink in, leaving me speechless. I don't know where to begin. Here he is, finally opening up, and I can't think of a word to say. Instead, I light a smoke. Click, Snap. We sit. We stare. We smoke. Silent. I focus on a tree growing between his trailer and his neighbor's. How could I have not noticed this tree before? It does not look natural—it looks too frail to be native to the land. It reminds me of Bill. Firmly planted in his own grief and regret, he's a tree that's been uprooted and replanted again and again. The roots are weak, tangled and weary. The tree may suffer terribly if you dare move it again, grown accustomed to its artificial space, yearning for permanence despite difficult conditions. I know he doesn't want to stay here. And I don't want him to die here. It's time to resume pushing.

"Dad, you need to get out more. Come visit us, find someone to watch Grandma for a bit. Meet your grandchildren; play with them, tell them stories, sing them songs. You said you would be happy if you could see your girls every week. You can. It's possible."

"It's hard to leave your grandma alone, you know. And besides, where would I go? What would I say?"

"Dad, do you think you're depressed? The way you're living would make anyone depressed."

"Yeah, probably. Sometimes I sleep from seven to ten at night, and then I'm up until three or four in the morning, I know that's not good. I'd like to get out more and do more things. I'm not getting any younger; I just don't know where to begin... I guess today I'll start by making lunch. Shoepeg corn, salisbury steak, some brownies maybe?" He shrugs. "Shoepeg corn makes me grumpy, I'm not crazy about it, but I had a coupon. Can you stay for lunch? Sorry I'm out of eggs, no breakfast today."

I will not let him escape this time. I will not talk about food or music or movies. It's time to push again, try a new angle. "Dad, what would you do if you could do anything? No boundaries, no limits, nothing to hold you back. Where would you go? What are your dreams? What do you think about when you're awake at night?"

He pauses, looks forward, tilts his head to the right and says, "I think about whales. I'd like to see the whales."

This of course is not the answer I'm seeking, or expecting.

"Yep, Care, I'd wish to see the whales in their natural habitat, just big fucking whales... can you imagine that?"

"Whales?"

"Oh yeah, it's my dream. Wouldn't mind seeing the Grand Canyon too… but number one on my list is the whales. In their big open fuckin spaces."

Shocked by the contrast of our conversation, all I can do is sigh.

"What, you got a better dream?"

In a twist of emotions, I resist the urge to laugh—an urge I assume is there to keep me from crying or screaming.

"You should contact Katie. You should make the first step. She was a little girl. You're a grown man. You're her father. I can get her number or address for you. Maybe you can write her a letter or something?"

"I'll think about it, I don't know Care." He taps his fingers along the chair, looks upward again and shrugs. He's considering an epidural, has had enough pushing for one day. Children are playing in the trailer park; we can hear them yelling, see them riding their bikes. A few look over at us, the whale and the midwife sitting in the plastic chairs. The shoulder shrug is what gets me. I cannot relate to his apathy, cannot wrap my head around the whales. Whales?

Defeated and exhausted, I swallow my frustration, stand and hug him instead of smacking him like I'd rather do. He asks when I'll be back, then tells me he'd like to meet my boys sometime. A sudden heat seeps through my body.

"I'll call you later this week." I kiss his cheek, in the exact spot I'd like to smack.

Funny how everything comes full circle. Now it's him waiting for my weekly visits, wondering if I'll show up. And it's me thinking, at this very moment, that maybe I'll never call him again.

Driving home, mind racing, Bill's playlist blaring, I do not hear my phone ring, but he has called and left me a message.

"Hey Care, it's Dad. I know you just left, but I just thought of something that's important to me. Do you realize I've seen you more in the last few months than I have in the last twenty years? Crazy huh? I love it. And I love you."

I save the voicemail because it's the first time he's called me in twenty years; the first time he's ever left me a message. Maybe he's practicing. Maybe, he's ready to resume pushing.

I can't help but smile.

Whales?

Breathe.

14
NEWTON'S LAWS
Soundtrack: "Tide Rushes In" – The Moody Blues

Newton's Laws are very simple.

Law #1 – Every object in a state of uniform motion tends to remain in that state of motion unless an external force is applied to it. Or, as more commonly known 'an object in motion stays in motion. An object at rest stays at rest.' Objects have a natural tendency to keep doing what they're doing. All objects resist change in their state of motion.

Bill, the wanderer, the dreamer, no longer moves. Bill sits outside. Dorothy sits inside. Bill's memories keep him planted. Dorothy's absence of memory works the same way.

Law #2 – The greater the mass, the greater the force needed to move it.

The alien baby is heavy.

Law #3 – For every action, there is an equal and opposite reaction. Newton's Cradle.

Bill and I had previously met in the center, touching and then splitting with greater force each occasion. What will happen this time? And where have Sir Newton's Laws landed me?

Through my late teens and most of my twenties, my thrice-divorced father moved once again back to Cincinnati, less than three miles away from us. I saw him every week, though he did not see me. He worked at a gas station, and I would drive by intentionally to catch a glimpse of the man I no longer knew. My little sister Twig was the one who told me he worked there. At the time she was attempting to forge a relationship with him—going to see him every so often, at which point he would typically ask to borrow money—but I couldn't bring myself to do the same. Still, I was curious, so I drove by often, slowing down and craning my neck to peer inside. Once I even stopped and filled my gas tank, watching him laugh with customers through the window, wondering if he could sense how near I was. He never did.

We continue our conversation from last week, resume pushing. I ask him about that mysterious decade, when he lived so close but never attempted to connect with me, with us. I want to know why, so I can keep it from happening again.

"I wanted to see you, but I knew you weren't happy with me, we hadn't spoken in so long. There was a time when Twig planned to bring your son over and I asked her to check with you first. She got back to me and said plans had changed, she wouldn't be bringing him over. That confirmed, for me, how you felt."

I do remember my sister asking if she could take my oldest son to meet his grandfather, and me telling her no way. I asked her to give him my phone number, to have him call me. He never did call. I didn't want my child to experience that same lifelong disappointment: Bill floating in and out, with no rhyme or reason. I didn't want him to meet my child, to give him a grandfather, and then leave. Start a motion and then stop it suddenly.

After our summer of Sundays, I still struggle with this. Could I risk allowing my sons to emotionally bond with their grandfather? Would that lead to healing or deeper hurt? I think I have forgiven him for what he did to me—but could I forgive again if he dealt them that same blow?

He gets a cigarette ready and resumes talking. I light one of my own and listen. "I told you I understood why you wouldn't want to see me, or have your son meet me. I still can't believe you're talking to me now. At the time there was nothing I could do to correct it, so I accepted it. I figured you were done with me, and who could blame you? I did what I knew best. I left."

Click, Snap. My mind is back in the therapist's room with my husband, staring at the floor, throwing my hands up, declaring "done" and leaving. My heart identifies with this motion.

"Did you know I used to drive by the gas station and see your face, see you working? Twig and I had friends who went there. They knew you were my dad and they would tell me they saw you. They would comment how friendly you were, how funny, how much we looked alike. It pissed me off that my friends could chat with you but I couldn't. Then, once again, you were gone. I went inside one day after not seeing your car for weeks and the man behind the counter told me you'd quit. And that was that. You vanished."

He begins telling me why he quit, his reasoning. How, it seems, he always quits. Poof. Gone. Click, Snap. My heart is in that gas station again, asking the strange man behind the counter about what happened to the guy who used to work there.

"Being a manager at the gas station was a pain in the ass. I had to constantly hire and fire people, stop people from stealing, and listen to them bitching about gas prices and their lives. As if I had anything to do with that. Anything and everything that went wrong was always my fault. But the job was only a mile away from home, and I had health insurance, so… I made it work. When the store was sold to a group of investors from India, I assumed my time was limited and gave my two-week notice. I had no plans for the future. Soon after I had to move—my rent was past due and my utilities were shut off."

"That's how you ended up living here with Dorothy?"

"No, I put all my stuff in storage and I found a place to sleep. My car. How's that, Care? How low can you get?"

I look over at the white Lincoln Town Car, dull

and dirty, sitting dead as lead in his driveway. It's the same car I looked for in the gas station parking lot. I picture him living in it, homeless, and I'm shocked by the lack of surprise, by how smoothly this piece fits into the puzzle.

We sit in our chairs and smoke, both staring at the vehicle he once called home.

"Wow. You lived in your car. For how long?"

"Let's just say, long enough. Another reason I didn't call. That's why I disappeared. I didn't have anything. That's quite a legacy to leave your children and grandchildren… part-time father turned homeless man. I felt lower than shit." He leans forward to stomp out his cigarette, his cough deep and wet. "And that's how I ended up out here. Grandma needed help and I had no other place to go. I told you some man bought the contents of my storage unit when I failed to pay. I literally had nothing. Sure it was a nice big car, but not comfortable to live in. My intentions weren't to stay in Blanchester. Now I have no choice. I'm stuck here." Like the chair. Like the trailer. Like the car.

I can't tell if his eyes are damp from tears, from coughing, or possibly amniotic fluid leaking. As he reaches for his next smoke, I'm wishing he would have called me, or that I had called him. Life is an endless series of what-ifs.

I ask about the alien baby. Like a crying child, it's begging for my attention, can no longer be ignored. "Some days I take ten to twelve Ibuprofens a day, Care. I feel a lump, I get a wrenching cough that causes a crunching—wretched sound—it started a few years ago. You know the alien baby is a joke, I kid because I have to, it hurts like hell sometimes, and the doctor is too expensive. I don't have health insurance, I don't have a car, or a driver's license even. I don't want to know what it is really, and I don't know how to stop the circle."

Again with his hands, they go up and spin around, like a record, like a song on repeat. My emotions course through me like turbulent weather: anger, sadness, compassion. I place my hand on his and hold it tight, to stop the circle and to let him know, silently, that I love him. We sit quietly together, between the trailers, in front of the immobilized car, in our little plastic chairs. I wonder who was the last person to hold his hand like this.

I squeeze a little. I love you.
He squeezes back. He can hear me.
We sit.

15
NEW BEGINNINGS, PART TWO
Soundtrack: "Daughters of the Soho Riots"–the
National

Another Sunday. Another trip to the grocery.
Another disposable talk with Dorothy while my
father cooks breakfast: eggs, of course.

Outside, we have our post-breakfast smoke. It's
late August, hot and moist. But like me, Bill prefers
the outdoor air. It feels real. "What's new, Care?"

"Nothin' much." I shrug and smile, and pluck
blades of grass from his parched yard.

On every drive home from my father's house, I
listen to his playlist. And each time I return home, I
take a shower. There's the obvious reason, to
shampoo the smoke out of my hair, but it's also to
rinse away the heavy weight of our collective
memories. This past week his regret clung to me,
screamed at me, demanded whether I was running

to or from something. I couldn't rinse it off. Newton's Laws gave me pause. I stumbled into simple yoga poses, ones I had done for many years, my mind racing, off balance. Where was I resisting motion? What force will propel movement? And what will the reaction to my actions be? What will I regret? How will the pendulum swing?

His regret clung, yet it was clarifying.

"Twig called yesterday. It had been awhile. I figured she called because of you, but she was surprised when I told her you'd been coming out to visit me. She had no idea."

Twig had called me too, right after talking to Bill. She couldn't believe I had been visiting our dad without telling anyone.

Now it's Bill's turn to stare. "What?" I ask, still toying with the grass, not looking up.

"Twig told me."

I suspected he'd already known, given the absence of a wedding ring and no mention of my husband. I toss a handful of dead grass. "No one's happy about it."

"Yeah, I got that. Twig told me you were crazy." He says it flippantly, but my jaw bones catch fire and my heart begins to melt all the same. I'm used to people staring at me: my mother, my sister, my friends, my soon-to-be ex. But not my dad. His stare breaks me. I start to cry.

His eyes widen. He's never seen me cry. "I'm sorry, honey. We don't have to talk about it. I'm not trying to be nosy." Click, Snap.

"It's all-right." Wiping my cheeks, I continue, "I need to talk. I need to cry. It's actually a good thing."

There, between the trailers, hidden from view by the white Lincoln Town Car, I finally release. Sure, I had cried about our separation before, usually in the bathroom with the shower running so the kids wouldn't hear. Or late at night, curled on the couch where I often slept, with a pillow pressed against my head to muffle the sound.

But I didn't cry when I told my husband it was time, nor when he agreed. The truth was, just like Bill, I didn't know how to be married; I didn't know how not to be married. I just knew how to leave.

Our friends were shocked. Our family was sad at first, then confused, then mad. They kept asking what the hell happened. "That's a loaded question," I would reply, offering no further explanation. They wanted someone to blame, some singular reason, a rational, clear-cut motive. In the absence of these things, they were rendered uncomfortable, vulnerable. As if divorce was a virus they could catch. Sometimes I would say, "It's private," an answer they hated. For years, we'd led them to believe our marriage was perfect, that I was perfect, and I felt like I was disappointing everyone by revealing we weren't immune, that we were flawed and failing. Every time I heard "I'm so sorry," I felt like I should be the one offering that sentiment.

We tried. We tried so hard, for nine years, had some beautiful times together. And I would do it all again.

Fixer and I had continued our lunches and walks throughout the summer, something we'd rarely done when we were together. On these walks, we had true conversations, because he no longer felt compelled to fix me and I no longer wanted him to.

We promised to be a team, to show the boys that we'd always be there for them, both of us, equally. We promised to respect each other always, as we'd once promised in our vows. We were going to cook the cracked and scrambled egg and turn it into a kind of feast, instead of letting it seep and pool and rot and stink. It's a testament to our characters that our divorce is exceptional, not ugly. That, I owe to Fixer, and his innate compassion. We still like each other. We're divorcing to keep it that way.

When he delivered our paperwork, he told me he was inspired to attach a thank-you note. "I was having lunch with my dad the other day, and I told him I feel as if I should thank you." We both laughed at this sentiment. How absurd. Thanking me. Fixer's dad is a Life Coach, which demonstrates the amazingness of genetics.

Fixer continued, "Seriously, though, a bright light has been shined into the dark corners of our marriage. I have experienced such growth in the past six months, experienced so many new things, and I believe---hope---you have too. This is all a huge change, but I like what I'm doing, where I'm going. There's nothing to be mopey about. And therein lies the gift of all of this." He swept his hands into the air, circling, a gesture I recognized because it belongs to me, and over the years he's adopted it. He ended our conversation by apologizing once again for calling me Bill's daughter, saying that he was truly sorry, it wasn't a nice thing to say. I told him it wasn't so bad.

"So, what happened, Care?"

"Oh, Dad, I don't know. Nothing happened. Everything happened. That's the problem. It's hard to explain. He was never around physically, I checked out emotionally. We let each other down I suppose, in our own separate ways. We lost our connection. It bothered me more than him."

"Did you guys try any counseling?"

"Yeah, we did. For a little bit. He moved out last March."

I smile and wipe away the tears, "You know, we could stay married, but it would be for the wrong reasons. We even thought about having an open marriage. He thought that would cure my lonely heart, satisfy my wandering spirit."

"They call that a loveless marriage."

"Eh, I've researched it; it works for some, I suppose. Who am I to judge? And our marriage wasn't loveless. It was good. We didn't fight. We didn't do anything intentionally to hurt each other. We just grew apart. Like I said, it's hard to explain."

"A lot of people stay together for various reasons, Care, almost like a partnership. Some can deal with it, are happy and content. Some stay just for sex. That's all they need. Others need that deeper connection. A mental, spiritual, lovey-dovey connection." He air quotes 'lovey-dovey'. "And it sounds like that's what you're missing, what you need."

"Absolutely." *Finally, someone understands.*

"Do you talk to anyone about it? Really talk?"

"Not really. I keep to myself for the most part. I focus on the boys, work, and get out and about when I can. I'm thankful. I focus on the good things. That's my mantra. I mean, there are a few friends I can talk to, be completely open with, but most don't understand. Most of my friends are 'our friends,' you know? It's tough. I don't like explaining myself anyway. Most of the time I probably don't make any sense." I continue, telling him about Kentucky, and our weekly emails. "I can't explain our connection, Dad. It's as simple as eggs and toast, and as complex as a Mahler symphony. Just like many things in life…" Bill listens, nods his head, doesn't question, and says, "Care, I'm happy to be one of those people you can go to, whenever you feel like talking. I'd like that, actually."

"Dad, have you ever heard of Rudolph Steiner, the philosopher? He has a theory that every seven years, we change significantly. Like, we leap into a new phase. I think there's some truth to that. I think I may be exiting one phase, entering the next."

"Nope, I've never heard of him, or that, but it sounds interesting."

"Yeah, that's actually where the term seven-year itch is derived from. Steiner's theory."

"Is there a philosopher who can explain the two-to-three-year itch, or one-night-stand itch? Because that was more my style." Click, Snap, smirk.

Shaking my head, "Not sure, Dad. I'll look into that. I think the one-night stand itch is something different entirely. And thanks. For saying you'll be there for me. I'd like that, too."

As we talk, a butterfly lands on my leg. We both pause to observe its wings flutter and flit, then watch as it flies away. "Okay. So… what do you think? You've been married a few times. Think this is the right choice we're making, or a big mistake?" As a woman, and as a child who never had the opportunity, I want to know what he is thinking, want to hear his advice.

"It's easier when you can put your finger on one big thing. Big things you can either agree to fix it or forget it. What's harder to handle is when the little problems grow. They're harder to see clearly, and then suddenly can't be ignored. Sounds to me that's what you're going through. That's no way to live, unless you just want to be partners. Or, you just need somebody to pick you up off the floor."

"True, though it is nice to be picked up sometimes."

"Yes it is. Never take that for granted." We both laugh, and he continues. "My god, Care, everybody's so complex and so different. It's a wonder any of us are here at all. Even though you're half of me there are so many things about us that are different. We may look alike, or talk alike, love our music and whatnot…but you seek things out. I run away. You're not afraid. You prove that every week by showing up here. I'm not that brave. You've shown me that we're very different. I wish I could be more like you."

"That's funny. You've shown me how we're much the same."

The butterfly circles, lands next to Bill for a moment, and then once again flies away. Bill follows it with his eyes, smiles and asks, "You see that butterfly? That's the same one that was on your leg. It keeps flying all around us."

"Yeah, I noticed that too. Wonder what that means."

Bill laughs, and then pauses. Click, Snap. Inhale, Exhale. "What what means?"

"You know, I'm sure having a butterfly hovering, circling, landing on you means something…" I reach out my hand for his Zippo.

Still amused, "Oh, Care, does everything have to mean something?" Then, shaking his head, he looks at me, and offers his theory. "I think it means you're a flower."

"Well, Dad," Click, Snap, "I guess that means you're a flower, too." He laughs. I lean back in my chair and try to blow my smoke away from the dancing butterfly. I don't want it to leave just yet, because maybe it's a sign that I'm blossoming.

I pop my head inside to say goodbye to Dorothy. She's in her chair, eyes fluttering awake from a nap, and she turns and looks at me. For a moment I think I see a flicker of recognition.

"Grandma, I'm sorry, did I wake you?"

"Oh, no, I had a nice little nap. I love my naps… In the meantime, it's such a great joy to wake up and see you here. You talk to me and everything." Chirp, chirp, chirp. I love her bird voice.

"Well, thanks Grandma. It's nice to see you

too." Closing her eyes, hovering somewhere between awake and dreaming, alive and dead, she carries on. "I wish you good luck. Take care and be careful, I love you, toodle-oo, good luck!"

Dorothy, the perennial planted in the chair. Perhaps she is a daisy; the name means "day's eye." The flower opens and closes with the sun, just like her. Every day brand-new, every yesterday forgotten.

My father, an apple blossom? The flower is a symbol of better things to come, yet the apple historically represents sin, seduction and war. But the apple, before the burden of its weight, is a pink blossom. A delicate, fragile color. The color of a newborn. The alien baby, pink and quiet, still hovering, has, thankfully, settled down a bit.

I don't know what flower I am. I'm fond of wildflowers. I once read that asters had healing powers, and I think that would be nice.

16
THEORY OF THE WHALES
Soundtrack: "Puff the Magic Dragon" – Peter, Paul and Mary

He is outside, smoking and sweeping leaves off the porch, waiting for us. We are late, but when he sees us, his smile is bright and forgiving.

"Well, well... look who's here."

I have hesitated long enough. He is a part of me, a part of them, and a good man. He needs to see them, make them eggs and such. The boys smile and look around, taking in the scenery, as I did many weeks ago. Sensing their uncertainty, Bill walks over, offers a handshake and asks, "Who the hell are you?" My youngest, Liam, looks at me, eyes wide, and grins. Logan stares at Bill, sizing him up.

Liam shakes Bill's hand, "I'm Liam." Bill replies, "I know. You're named after me. William... Liam... didn't your mom tell you that?" Liam was indeed not named after Bill, but I recognize his strategy, his default charm and wit. I look at Liam; we both roll our eyes and smile.

Logan isn't so easy, and Bill senses this. Approaching him, he says in a very serious tone, "Sorry to say, Logan, I'm certain you're not named after me." Logan cracks half a smile and shakes his grandpa's hand.

"Need some help with that?" Bill asks, peering into my Volvo. Along with my children, I brought my laptop, so we could watch the "35th But Feels Like 50th" birthday DVD. "You ever clean this car out?"

"My car's a mess, Dad. Get over it. I live in my car."

He's mumbling 'what is all this shit...' still peering in the windows, ignoring my overloaded arms and poor choice of words.

"This shit is some work stuff, pool stuff, school stuff, stuff stuff...."

"That's right, you cut hair." He comes around to the open hatchback, starts rifling through my belongings, picks up a binder of poems that have slipped open. "Is this yours? Do you write poetry?" I had recently joined a writing group. They meet on Friday nights, perfect for a lonely 35-year-old with an abundance of time and feelings to unload.

"Yeah, I've been writing poems and stuff." I grab the papers from his hands as he tries to read them, irritated by his familiar smirk.

"Well, maybe you could give me a haircut some time, read me some of your poems... hey, are you guys hungry? I made some chili." Turning to the boys, who have wandered off to get a closer look at Bill's parked car, he shouts, "You guys like chili?"

"They've never had chili, Dad." They both look nervous, and I mouth "just try it" as we walk inside the trailer, laptop and birthday DVD in hand.

Dorothy sits in her favorite chair, an old wingback model from the sixties. During our drive to Blanchester, I explained to the boys that she was old, and sweet. I tried to explain how Alzheimer's is like waking up each day brand-new, that their great-grandmother doesn't remember much of anything, past or present.

After brief introductions she offers the boys cookies, making them fast friends, and they take turns playing on her mechanical recliner. The chair was free courtesy of Medicare. She never sits in it.

"How's your mom, by the way?" Dad asks me while preparing our lunch.

"She's good. Why?"

"I was going to call her the other day, and thought it would be funny if when she picked up I said 'what are you wearing?'— just leave it at that. I thought, now that would be funny."

"You should, she'd know it was you. And it would be funny… I can just imagine her face." She would shit if he called her.

"Yeah, I was gonna call her, then for some reason, didn't."

He places three plates and all the fixings for chili cheese coneys on the table. The boys aren't sure what to do with this concoction. Even though we live in Cincinnati, they've never eaten

Cincinnati chili. Bill explains to the boys how to eat
a coney—how to add onions, mustard, cheese,
etc.—and then lectures me for not raising them
right. "How can they never have had a coney,
Carrie, what the hell's wrong with you?" He then
launches into a story.

"I bet you guys are wondering how I got out
here, why I'm living out here. And by the way, if
you have any suggestions on how to get the hell out,
feel free to share them." He has seen them looking,
observing. Wide-eyed Liam giggles, cueing Bill to
proceed. He has his audience.

"When I was younger I created this amazing
chili recipe you're about to eat. I worked so hard, a
little dash of this, a little dash of that, until I got it
just right you see. And I started making it for
friends. And then one day this man comes up to me
and he says, "Bill, I hear you make some fine chili."
So I told him my recipe and he went off and opened
up a restaurant with my chili recipe. Didn't give me
a cent. So, here I sit. That man's rich off my chili.
Can you believe that?"

"That must suck!" Liam believes his story.
Logan is still staring at the ground beef; he doesn't
buy it. Liam glances at the brown and yellow blob
in front of him and fearlessly requests a grilled
cheese, which Bill makes without hesitation. Logan
eats the cheese coneys, but spends the latter part of
the evening back home, on the toilet, with
hellacious diarrhea and stomach pains, cursing my
father's famous chili.

"I thought we could watch the '35th But Feels

Like 50' DVD and then go to the grocery if you need to." I plug in my laptop and get the movie ready. The boys are back on the mechanical recliner, entertaining Dorothy.

"Hey Care, I've been thinking of this song idea, maybe you could help me. You see, I have this idea of a man and woman talking, but only the man's voice is really speaking. Her voice, the woman's, is an echo... almost like the man is in a canyon, but he's not really, and he's thinking and she's replying. It sounds like an echo is answering his thoughts. He's not sure where the echo's coming from, he just hears... this voice, this answer, an echo. Then he sings, the chorus could be, *all I hear is an echo...*" Whatcha think?"

I like the idea, I can see where he is going, but already I'm reading into it too much. I picture him lying awake at night, thinking of all the things he'd still like to say, hearing only the echo of the answers he longs for. Much like the echoes that I listened for back on my rock, in the hills of Kentucky. I believe the echo he's hearing has been me all along.

But maybe that's just me, hunting down metaphors, always searching for a meaning.

"I like it, Dad, I think it's interesting. Why don't you work on it, write some lines down, see where it takes you, and I'll do the same?"

"Alright, I'll do that. We should definitely write a song together. Hell yeah. Hey, did your mom ever tell you about the time we went and saw Neil Diamond together? We had terrible seats ... your mom was so cute; somehow she got us moved up to like the eighth row or something. That was a good concert. We saw him live once, and John Gary. Ask her about John Gary. I think those are the only two concerts we saw together." Click, Snap. Now he's smoking and cussing in front of the boys, but I say nothing.

He's mentioned my mom twice today. I realize they had this beautiful time together, a life together, about which I still know so little. Today he's remembering the little things, the happy times. I realize he still knows very little about me, the happy times, the sad times, the trifling moments. This DVD may be a nice introduction.

Adjusting the screen and volume, I overhear Bill ask the boys if I have any photos of whales on my birthday DVD. "You know what, if I'd sold my chili recipe I would have taken the money and gone to see the whales swimming."

"That's so random." Logan's voice. He's hardly said a word.

"Yep, kids, that's my dream. Just big goddamn whales. In their big open spaces. Can you imagine that?"

"Hey Dad, no whales on here, but are you ready to watch my life on a twenty minute DVD? There's even a soundtrack."

First, he marvels at my laptop. Then Dad, Grandma, the boys and I gather around to watch the slideshow that's set to some music my mom picked out. The opening song? Yep. "Carrie Anne."

Dorothy smiles and comments on how cute the kids are; sadly, she doesn't recognize a young Bill and is unable to connect the people on the screen with the same ones standing right in front of her.

My dad watches closely and quietly, with the occasional laugh. There are photos of him, a few of the four of us—Mom, Dad, Twig and I, together. Many others are from my high school years, when he was markedly absent—and, truthfully, I was too. There are photos of my children through the years, and of my once perfect family, my perfect house. When those appear I watch my children, looking for any clues of hidden emotions. As I look back and forth from my children to my father, suddenly it hits me: my oldest son is a mirror image of my father. Same eyes, same jawline, same smile. They both stand watching the screen with their hands in their pockets—same posture, same mannerisms, same wonderstruck grins. How could I have missed this?

Per Bill's request, we watch it twice. Afterward, I show him more photos on my computer. He is thoughtful and curious, especially focusing on the pictures of my boys.

Hungry for what he's been missing.

The moment we can no longer see him waving goodbye, the boys unleash their inquiries. "Mom, do you think they sell drugs in his neighborhood? Is that what it's called? It's still a neighborhood, right?'

"Technically, Logan, it's a trailer park community, which is just like a neighborhood. And drugs can be sold anywhere."

"Seems really boring," Logan adds. "But, I don't know, I might want to be like him when I grow up. He's nice, he's not boring, just his house is. You know what they say, mo' money mo' problems…" Logan does his best rap face.

"You'd want to sit around smoking all day and have to live with that old lady?" Liam asks.

"Dude, that's his freaking mother."

"Hey! Just because Bill cusses, don't you start. I know what 'freaking' means."

"Oh my God, he said the F bomb twice. Freaking hilarious." Logan smiles as he remembers his grandpa, who has certainly made an impression. "I like him. He's funny. You guys are nothing alike."

"I beg your pardon. I'm funny." *I'm fucking funny.*

"Yeah, sorta… but you don't really cuss or anything."

"You guys have the same eyes. And face. And you chew your food the same." Liam is now sharing his observations. "He is funny. He seems sad, though. Downhill."

"Downhill? What does that mean?"

"Downhill, you know, like downhill…" Liam makes quotes in the air. "Depressing…"

"What's with the whale thing? That was so freaking random. You'd think he'd be like, 'gee, I'd like to get out of this trailer.' Or, 'man, I miss my family'…" Logan and Liam both laugh, and then Logan adds, "Yeah, I think he's smart. And the whales could be a metaphor for something."

Yes, just as I was thinking…

"Boys, tell you what. When we get home, let's research whales. Check out symbolism, philosophy, use of whales in story and songs… see if we can find some reason, some hidden meaning, for his wish." They groan, but do indeed join me in research, as soon as we arrive home.

17
SAVOR
Soundtrack: "Oh Very Young" – Cat Stevens

Again, he waits for me outside on a Sunday morning. Faded jeans, white button-down short-sleeve shirt, white sneakers. Will he forever dress like an aging folk singer?

I dig through my car, collecting the haircutting tools that have spilled across my backseat. "Hey Dad, how's it goin? Wanna get your hair cut today?" Throughout the summer his hair has taken on a life of its own, and not in a good way. As a hairstylist, I felt compelled to offer him a haircut. As his daughter, I wanted to seize the opportunity to meet this obvious need, because I could.

"That'd be great, Care. Think you could cut Grandma's too?"

"Of course. I planned on it."

I set down my backpack of necessities—combs

and trimmers, a cape, mirror, scissors—and take a seat on the ground.

"Ahhh, what a beautiful day, huh Care." He reaches for a smoke. In the sunlight, his hair glows like a halo. Saint Bill.

"You excited for your haircut? Just so you know, I'm not half bad."

Click. Snap. Smoke swirls, Saint Bill on fire. "Sure I am. Did you eat breakfast? I got some eggs." He emphasizes eggs with his eyebrows. He reminds me of Einstein.

After breakfast, I start with Grandma's cut, so she can take her nap. Her thin hair hangs limp and long around her face, well past her shoulders, gray and neglected. I ask how she's been, and she replies, "Oh, fat and sassy as usual." As I begin to cut, I wonder when was the last time someone told her she was pretty, so I do. She laughs off the compliment with a wave of her hand.

Cutting someone's hair has its practical purposes, but for me it can feel quite spiritual. As I shampoo someone, massage their scalp, I can feel the weight of their day dissipate. I love it when people Zen out, honor the ritual. Listening to my clients, just being present in the moment with them, it often occurs to me that I may be the only person to touch them, to truly hear them, for that entire day. Maybe even longer. They leave, feeling and looking better, having no idea how they've touched me. I talk to lots of people. I listen to heartwarming stories, dirty jokes, deep secrets, personal thoughts. I love this part of my job, the human connections

I've grown to crave.

Midway through her haircut, Grandma begins to coo, talking to me longer than she ever has before. She calls me Love. She giggles like a toddler, her voice a bird's tweet. "Love, I just want you to know I'm so happy you talk to me, I'm fond of all the nice things you do and say. Thank you for being nice to me." I finish her haircut—dry and style her hair gently—then give her a hug as she shuffles over to her chair for a nap.

Now it's Bill's turn. "Dad, it's time for you to lose this hairdo. You look like Doc from Back to the Future."

"Should I trust you?"

Should he trust me? Doesn't everyone wonder that when someone new cuts their hair for the first time? I get his joke, though. He worries I've been plotting my revenge all summer.

"You can trust me; I've been doing this forever." It's true; I used to color my mom's hair when I was eight, when she couldn't afford a salon. I'd sit on a chair, pulling strands of her hair through a cap and painting on bleach, as she sat on the floor. I played with my cousin's hair, colored Barbie hair with Kool Aid, styled all my friends' hair for proms and parties. I got my first job in a salon when I was fifteen—answering phones, folding towels, but mostly listening and observing.

I fasten the cape and spray his hair with warm water. Like most people, he settles in. His wet hair hangs to his shoulders. Relaxed, he starts chatting. "How's everything going? You doin' alright? Still gettin' a divorce?"

As I'm professionally groomed to do, I follow his lead. "Yeah, we met up yesterday, paperwork bullshit, stuff like that. I'm not really good with the fine print. We should have everything finalized by October, I guess. I'm amazed at how easy getting a divorce can be. It's nice, I guess, but shouldn't be so easy."

"You doin' okay?"

"You've asked me that twice now. Yeah, I'm fine. Are you?"

"How are the boys?"

"Oh, they're amazing. They say hello, by the way. I'll bring them with me again sometime soon. Nice bullshit story about the chili. They're telling everybody how their grandpa got robbed."

"So, still getting a divorce, life's good, boys are good. This is none of my business, but is Fixer dating anybody?"

"Why do you ask?"

"Well, I don't know, I don't mean to be nosy, but divorces seem to move a lot faster when, you know, either party has some company." Never faithful in marriage, he speaks from experience.

"Well, you know, he moved out almost six months ago, so... we don't really talk about it, but he has mentioned having a date and stuff like that. I don't know the details and whatnot, but we're moving on. If he is dating, I'm glad. I just want him to be happy. "

"Are you?"

"What, happy or dating?"

"Both."

I ponder what to say. When I was younger,

starting to date, I imagined having my dad around to talk to. I would have loved for him to ask if I was happy, tell me a boy was off limits, or that I was too young, too good, and maybe too pretty or smart for just anybody. Of course, most likely I would have defied him, but it would have been nice to have that conversation.

"Yeah…I'm happy, and I am dating a little."

"And…"

"I'm afraid." There, I said it. After well over a decade, dating was foreign territory, riddled with land mines.

"What are you afraid of?"

I flip my shears around and point to my chest, fake stab myself, laugh and act like I'm dying. "I don't know, Dad, I feel like a lot of people don't want to hear, or believe, that I'm happy. Maybe I don't even know how to recognize happiness, or accept it. I feel like I'm not even allowed to say it. When you're getting divorced you're supposed to be angry or sad, right? People keep saying they're sorry, and I don't know how to respond to that."

"You can talk to me, honey. Remember, I'm happy to be one of those people you can talk to, not just cuz I'm bored as hell out here. I might tell Grandma just because I'm bored, ya' know… but shit, she won't tell anybody. You still talk to your friend in Kentucky?"

"Yeah. Pretty much every day. Why?"

"Oh I don't know. I guess it depends on what you talk about. Or, more importantly, in your case, what you don't say."

He continues. "So, let's talk about this fellow

you're dating. How'd you meet? Plenty-o-fish dot com or something? What's he like? What's he do for a living? Are you dating random people, or just one?" The questions tumble out, a flood of curiosity. He's imagined this conversation before, too.

"I'm not dating random people, as you put it, which is awkward by the way... but I am happy seeing this one gentleman now." Somewhere between the Indian takeout and stargazing, Shakespeare and I had begun dating. Slow and without expectations, Shakespeare likened us to us 1950's romance. I told him my nickname for him was 'Savor', for I was enjoying the relaxed moments, the break from the sadness, knowing full well eventually one of us would leave.

"He's a teacher, and an actor. He's very interesting. We're taking it slow. And no, I didn't meet him on plenty-o-fish. I've actually known him a few years. So, do you want me to cut your hair or not? I kinda need to concentrate."

"Taking it slow, huh? That's good. I should have tried that at least once. And honey, you should know better than to date an actor."

"Yeah, okay. Thanks for the tip." I let his comment fall to the floor along with his hair.

"You know Dad, you could still try taking it slow... especially now with this handsome haircut. You should call Mom." I have this vision of my parents falling in love again, though I know that's not likely to happen. At the very least, I'd like them to be friends.

I have to stop cutting when he laughs, his entire

body shaking with amusement at the thought of dating somebody. "Honey, there ain't nobody to date out here! I always loved your mom. How is she?"

"Jesus, Dad, sit still. Mom's great. You should call her and ask her what she's wearing."

But he can't stop laughing, continues shaking his head from side to side. "That's right, I was gonna do that. That would be funny. That's good, Care. Taking it slow is good too. Not like the 70's... whew... those were some days. So, what's this fellow's name?"

"Shakespeare." He laughs so hard I nip my finger. He dashes into the bathroom and emerges holding a box of bandages he's labeled OUCH. "So you're dating Shakespeare. That's fancy. As he wraps the bandage around my knuckle, I lean in close and whisper, "You know, his name isn't really Shakespeare. How about we just call him Savor, as in taking it slow..."

"Oh, I like that... like Salisbury Steak!" I refasten the cape around his neck and resume my purpose. "Savor, huh. I see where you're going. Fine, don't tell me his name, just cut my hair, not your fingers. And I'm old, hurry up." He snaps his fingers, repeats, "I'm old!"

I take my time cutting his hair, savoring.

Bill breaks the silence. "Care, stop for a second, I got something to say, this is important, are you listening?" I stop and stand in front of him, staring straight into his eyes.

"Don't be ashamed to feel, or tell people, that

you're happy. Or that you love them. And Care?"

"Yeesss…" I turn to look him in the eye again. "Men aren't mind readers." I smile, he winks, and returns an affectionate, yet weary, grin.

Love advice, from Dad.

"Hey, guess what? I'm learning to play the guitar, and when Savor Salisbury Steakspeare gets back in town I'm going to play him a song. I'm even going to sing." Logan's helping me learn, along with YouTube videos. It's brutal. I'm terrible. But it's a better diversion than drinking and smoking when I'm alone at the still unfamiliar apartment.

"Oh no, Carrie… that's going too fast. How about you play guitar, and I'll sing?" He cringes a little. I see it in his shoulders.

"Watch it, I have scissors next to your ear. This is a big fuckin' deal, Dad. I'm actually afraid to sing, like really sing, in front of anyone. You know, you told me once I sang in monotone." I slap him across the shoulder. "That's why I'm doing it. Because I'm afraid. Do what you're afraid to do, right?"

"Something like that," he replies, holding back a fresh round of laughter. "And honey, you sing great—hell yeah, go ahead and sing. I'd tell ya' if you really stunk. You were just going through puberty. Voice was all shaky."

He remembers. "You always used to sing. All day long, when you were a little girl. I like it when you sing."

"I like it when *you* sing."

"Yeah, I like myself when I sing."

"Do you think this is a bad idea? Be honest. Shakespeare asked me recently what my biggest fear was. I didn't admit I had two, one of which is singing... you know, singing with someone actually listening. I don't know, I think it's gonna be great. Or, at the very least, hilarious."

"Well, that's a good attitude. Let me know how it goes. Just tackle one fear at I time. Your other fear is admitting you're happy, right? That way if he bolts when you start singing, you'll have knocked two fears out in one day."

"I'm not taking your advice anymore if you're going to make fun of me. And by the way, my other fear is not the happy thing. It's that." I point my shears toward the doily-laced freaky alien baby head still hanging in the kitchen.

"Yeah, I'm afraid of that too."

"So, Care, I've been thinking more about my echo song idea. I can't put into words what I'm hearing in my head, but I want to write a song about echoes."

"I've been thinking about that too. And your whale obsession."

"Oh yeah?"

"Yeah. The boys and I did some research. Did you know whales symbolize creativity, intuition, death, rebirth, and circles of life?"

"No shit."

"Yeah, and of course, in the Bible Jonah was vomited by a whale."

"I don't want that to happen."

"It's a metaphor, Dad—more rebirth, resurrection..."

"Mmmm, hmmm… okay..."

"You've heard of Sinbad, right? Well, he got stranded on the back of a whale, thought it was an island."

"Yep. Been there."

"Here's some good stuff you'll dig… whales also symbolize the power of song, voice, knowledge, and movement. And did you know statues of the Buddha often have whales on them?"

"No, I did not know that. Are you a Buddhist?"

"As far as your echo idea, whales are supposed to teach us to hear our inner voice, our echo, you see? A whale's song echoes throughout the ocean."

He begins to sing. "And all I hear is an echo…"

"Yep. See…"

"So, it all means something, huh Care?

"Well, you know…"

"Ok, so, not to change the subject, but how is it possible that half the people I talk to don't like Abba? Don't tell me you don't like Abba. How can anybody not like Abba?"

"I don't know, Dad." I don't admit that I'm not a fan of Abba myself.

"Let me ask you something else. Think they'll ever run out of words? Do you think people will just eventually run out of songs to write, all the words will have been used in all the ways possible and then they'll stop making new songs?"

"No, Dad. That will never happen. Humans will always find the words, write the lyrics, sing the songs, play the music. That I know for sure. We would die as a species if we didn't have music to get us through life."

"Hey, that reminds me. I have a new list of songs I was hoping you could burn for me. That's it, right there on the counter. There's some Abba on there. And I really want the long version of 'Jump' by the Pointer Sisters."

I brush the hair off his shoulders and pick up his list. This one is happier, lighter. "You mean there's a long version of 'Jump'?" I thought it was long enough already.

"Yeah, has a killer intro. You know why I want the long version?"

"No."

"Because I already have the short one."

We cackle like a couple of old drunks.

His haircut and our conversation finished, I remove the cape and he looks like a new man. He admires himself in the mirror as I sweep the floor and pack up my things. I pick up his latest playlist off the counter, replace it with a few of my poems for him to discover and read later. "Good job, Care. I don't look half bad. Hell, I look great. Maybe I will go get myself a cute girlfriend. Maybe I'll call your mom, see what she's wearing. Hey, ask her about the yellow dress sometime."

Snapping his fingers, dancing around his living room, humming, Click, Snap, inhaling, exhaling… "Hey Care, I'm serious, let's write that song about echoes. Echoes and whales and whatnot." His hands rise to the heavens and then float back down, encompassing the room, like he's catching the wind. He may not have found the right words yet, but he can already hear the music.

I watch with a smile as he spins, stops, and then with jazz hands and a wink, exclaims…

"Whaddaya say!?"

EPILOGUE
Soundtrack: "One Little Song" – Gillian Welch

On August 9th, 2011, Bill died in his sleep.

Twig received the call. His siblings knew she was the one who always reached out. None of them knew how to find me. Like Bill, I was the elusive one.

During the year leading up to Bill's death, the boys and I visited him often. Once my solo pilgrimage was complete, I wanted my children to know their grandfather. I wanted my dad to replace his "Sunday Morning Coming Down" with a new song. He told my boys inappropriate jokes and stories, fed them food of questionable quality, smoked and cussed and made them smile. In their presence, he could laugh without coughing, and sing without crying.

Eventually Bill began to pull away again. Our visits became less and less frequent, and then they stopped. I would call every Sunday to see how he was doing, and he would tell me he wasn't feeling good, wasn't in the mood for visitors. Perhaps he knew he was dying and didn't want his decline to be what I remembered most clearly. I followed his wishes, let him be. In that respect, Bill and I are a lot alike. When we say we need space, when we say we are done—we do, and we are. Yet I still called every Sunday, if only so he would hear the phone ring.

The morning of August 10th, 2011, I printed out the first rough draft of this book. I put it in a binder and attached a sticky note: "Dad's copy." I stuck another note on my bathroom mirror, reminding me to "Call Dad" before work. As I stepped out of the shower that Tuesday morning, my phone was ringing. When I saw that I'd missed four calls from Twig, I knew.

On auto-pilot, I went to work. I stared at my schedule, my mind drifting without direction. Twig needed me at Bill's house. My clients needed me at the salon. I needed to drive with no destination, with music as my only companion. Instead, I cancelled my appointments and met Twig at Bill's. We sat together in his tiny bedroom, reminiscing and sorting his things, until the smell of death crept in like fog, forcing us out.

On his bedside was a notebook—a fresh playlist, more songs he wished to hear. The music was upbeat, hinting at a new state of mind: "Jump" by Van Halen, "Night Fever" by the Bee Gees, "Hold Me, Thrill Me, Kiss Me" by Mel Carter; Hot Chocolate's "You Sexy Thing," "To Be Loved" by

Jackie Wilson, "Street Fightin Man" by the Rolling Stones, and "The Lion Sleeps Tonight" by the Tokens were just a few of the selections. Next to the song "It's My Turn" by Diana Ross, he'd scribbled, all caps, "CARE, THIS SONG'S FOR YOU."

Later that day, I went to the pool, craving solitude and warmth, needing to be alone while this new reality of Life Without Bill settled into my bones and my brain. I told myself it shouldn't be much different—after all, he'd been absent for much of my life anyway so it should be an easy transition, right? I was fooling no-one. I put on my headphones. I pulled up a chair beside mine, a place for him to sit, and a table for his martini.

Bill had lived and dreamed through music. We always had that connection, and we have it still. He lives on. He speaks to me through song. I just have to pay attention.

Bill was cremated. I drove alone to pick up the ashes, entered the empty funeral home and saw the box on the table. Someone had written my name on a post-it and attached it to the box. It was surreal, seeing my name attached to Bill's remains—and oddly comforting, too.

Surprised by the weight of his ashes, I sat down on the floor and cried. I'm not sure how much time passed. When I finally returned to my car, Twig had called, asking if I was okay. Apparently it's not common practice to pick up your father's ashes alone. I turned on my stereo and hit shuffle on my i-pod. As I drove, Beck's "Guess I'm Doing Fine" began to play, my father's remains beside me on the passenger seat. Someday I hope to scatter them alongside the whales.

We held a small memorial for Bill in October, two months after his death. My mom poured herself into the details, putting together a photo collage and making memory books for Twig and me. She was grieving her one true love. When I asked how she was feeling, she gave her forever reply, "I always loved your father"—only this time adding, "He filled the room."

None of Bill's friends attended the memorial. In fact, I'm pretty sure Bill, at the end, had no true friends. He was a complicated man. If you'd known Bill for any length of time, odds are he had broken your heart, screwed you over, or simply left. You wanted to be near him, but didn't know why. When he left—and he always left—his reasons would be a mystery. That was his way.

A few of Bill's brothers and sisters came. Stepping back and listening to their stories made me mourn what I missed growing up. My dad's side of the family is a colorful crew. I would have liked to have known them better. The majority of the attendees were my and Twig's friends and co-workers, and members of our mother's family—well, except for Mammaw. Though she still slept beneath a dying Jesus, she declined her invitation, stating she could never forgive Bill for his sins.

A week after Bill's death, Dorothy had a new home in a nursing facility. My heart ached as I imagined her confusion. Was she aware that her son had died? Did she search for him, call for him? Or was God kind enough to release her last sliver of memory when Bill took his final breath? I want to visit Dorothy—take her cookies, comb her hair, hold her hand—but I never have. I can't. I don't know why. For this, I am ashamed.

When Twig called to tell me about the contents of the coroner's report, she began with, "His heart was twice the size that a human heart should be." That was all I needed to hear. For once in my life, I didn't search for the reason or the meaning. For me, it was clear. The alien baby had lived in his heart until it was finally born, releasing Bill from captivity. Everyone else would recognize that he'd suffered a heart attack, sometime between taking out the trash Monday night and failing to turn off his TV in the wee hours of an August Tuesday morning.

I believe our summer of Sundays released Bill from the pain he suffered, released him from the alien baby, and diminished his regret. This belief, real or imagined, comforts me. My time with Bill was a gift, a unique opportunity for us to understand one another. There was little that wasn't said, or silently shared in the quiet spaces. Everyone should be so lucky.

The cover photo for this book was taken by Bill in the month and year of my birth. It shows my hill, home to my rock. The fact that my dad took a photo of my haven and retreat, my meditation, my center, just days before I was born—it can't be a coincidence.

Reconciliation is to understand both sides; to go to one side and describe the suffering being endured by the other side, and then go to the other side and describe the suffering being endured by the first side.
– Thich Nhat Hanh

BONUS TRACK
England—The National

How do you write a love letter to a band? To people you've never met, but who---through melodies and poetry---have written the soundtrack to your life? Coincidentally (and by now, you must know I don't believe in coincidence...) in the early to mid 2000s I met a woman while out walking my dog. She lived down the street. Her sons were in a band, living in Brooklyn. She told me she felt like they were on the cusp of something big. She mused, as all mothers do, about choices and dreams, supporting those you love, and how all she wanted was for her boys to be happy. I told her it was awesome she supported their dreams and honored their gift. I'd see her occasionally. We'd wave, say hello, suburban courtesies… I'd ask her how her boys were doing and she'd ask me about mine. Then, she and I both, moved away.

As it turns out, her boys went on to record an album that changed my life forever and perfectly

mirrored my experience of 2010. The National's
High Violet.

Small world, big universe.

Thank you to the members of The National—
Matt Beringer, Bryce and Aaron Dessner (say hello
to your mother for me), Bryan Devendorf and Scott
Devendorf—I know at least one of you has to be a
Dreamer like me. Your music brings me comfort,
makes me feel a little less lonely and a little more
understood. The first time I listened to you, I had to
sit down, close my eyes, and absorb, for that is what
I was taught to do when beautiful music takes over
a space.

Thank you.

And, feel free to write a song about echoes and
whales and whatnot…

ABOUT THE AUTHOR

Carrie Herzner is a mother, writer, hairstylist, yoga devotee and Dreamer. She resides in Cincinnati, Ohio

For more photos, excerpts, and music, visit
www.carrieherzner.com